MOON METRO

CONTENTS

ROME

HOW TO USE THIS BOOK

MAP SECTION

- We've divided Rome into seven distinct areas. Each area has been assigned a color, used on the map itself and in easy-to-spot map number indicators throughout the listings.

- The maps show the location of every listing in the book, using the icon that indicates what type of listing it is (sight, restaurant, etc.) and the listing's locator number.

- The coordinates (in color) indicate the specific grid that the listing is located in. The black number is the listing's locator number. The page number directs you to the listing's full description.

MAP 3 TRIDENTE

LISTINGS SECTION

- Listings are organized into six sections:

  ★ SIGHTS

  ℝ RESTAURANTS

  ℕ NIGHTLIFE

  ⑤ SHOPS

  ⓐ ARTS AND LEISURE

  ⓗ HOTELS

- Within each section, listings are organized by which map they are located in, then in alphabetical order.

LA ROSETTA   TAZZA D'ORO   GINA

RICCIOLI AFTER HOURS • INTERNATIONAL $$
If Massimo Riccioli's La Rosetta is too steep for your budget, head around the corner to his more casual but terminally chic bar/restaurant. Japan meets Italy in this mod space, serving sushi, oysters, and seafood to Fendi-wearing hipsters and body-conscious it-girls until 2 AM.

A4 ℝ 12   PIAZZA DELLE COPPELLE 10A
06-68-21-03-13

LA ROSETTA ROMANTIC • SEAFOOD $$$
This elegant, high-class restaurant is considered one of the best for fish in the entire city. Tasting menus are the best way to experience the kitchen's range, which spans simple grilled catch to light pastas with shellfish. All are delicious and unimaginably fresh.

B4 ℝ 30   VIA DELLA ROSETTA 8
06-68-61-002

SALOTTO 42 CAFE $
Salotto is Italian for "living room," appropriate for the library-chic decor and novella-sized menu of teas, coffee drinks, and cocktails. And it's a room with a view: Gaze across to the 2nd-century Temple of Hadrian from your comfy sofa cushion.

B4 ℝ 35   PIAZZA DI PIETRA 42
06-67-85-804

SANTA LUCIA HOT SPOT • ITALIAN $$
Almost all the seats here are outdoors under mature trees decorated with lights. The food is equally creative, light, and mostly healthy, with small course options for those who don't want a huge meal. Fish dishes from the Amalfi Coast is a specialty.

A2 ℝ 8   LARGO FEBO 12
06-68-80-24-27

TAZZA D'ORO CAFE $
Competing with Caffè Sant'Eustachio for the Best-in-Rome title, Tazza d'Oro packs in serious coffee drinkers – many of them politicos from the nearby senate building – who down espresso standing up at the bar. The coffee granita (shaved ice) with homemade whipped cream is a must.

B5 ℝ 33   VIA D'ORFANI 84
06-67-89-792

28 MOON METRO

TWO WAYS TO NAVIGATE

1. Scan the map to see what listings are in the area you want to explore. Use the directory to find out the name and page number for each listing.

2. Read the listings to find the specific place you want to visit. Use the map information at the bottom of each listing to find the listing's exact location.

⊙ SIGHTS

A2 **1** Piazza del Popolo, p. 10
B6 **16** + Villa Borghese, p. 8
C2 **19** Ava Paris, p. 9
C2 **20** Mausoleo di Augusto, p. 10
C5 **29** + Piazza di Spagna, p. 8
F5 **73** + Fontana di Trevi, p. 5

⊙ RESTAURANTS

A2 **2** Ristorante dal Bolognese, p. 31

B3 **9** Il Brillo Parlante, p. 29

D3 **30** Recafè, p. 30
D4 **39** Roman Garden Lounge, p. 30
D5 **42** Babington's Tea Rooms, p. 29
D5 **48** Da Mario, p. 29
E2 **52** El Toulà, p. 29
D3 **53** Obikà, p. 30
D3 **54** Matricianella, p. 30
D3 **55** Non Solo Bevi, p. 30
E3 **60** Hamasei, p. 30
F5 **71** Il Gelato di San Crispino, p. 29

⊙ NIGHTLIFE

A3 **5** Stravinskij Bar at Hotel de Russie, p. 42
B6 **17** Art Café, p. 41
E5 **59** Gilda, p. 41

⊙ SHOPS

B2 **7** Buccone, p. 53
D3 **8** L'Olfattoria Bar a Parfums, p. 56
D3 **11** Merola, p. 55
B3 **12** Discount dell'Alta Moda, p. 53
B3 **14** TAD, p. 56
C3 **21** Il Messaggerie, p. 55
C3 **22** The Lion Bookshop, p. 55
C4 **24** Almarì, p. 52
C4 **26** Eleonora, p. 53
C4 **27** AVC by Adriana Campanile, p. 52
D3 **32** Pineider, p. 56
D3 **33** Via Condotti/Via dei Corso, p. 57
D4 **34** Mariella Burani, p. 55
D4 **35** H. Martinelli, p. 55
D4 **36** Sermoneta Ties, p. 56
D4 **37** Battistoni, p. 52
D4 **38** Valentino, p. 56
D4 **40** Fausto Santini, p. 54
D4 **41** Fornari, p. 54
D5 **46** Femme Sistina, p. 54

D5 **47** Testa, p. 54
D5 **49** Francesco Biasia, p. 54
E3 **56** Bottega Veneta, p. 53
E3 **57** Profumeria Materozzoli, p. 56
E5 **58** Anglo-American Book Co., p. 52
F2 **66** Enrico Camponi, p. 53
E7 **67** Gioielli In Movimento, p. 55
F6 **68** Frette, p. 54
F4 **69** Rizzoli, p. 56
F6 **70** Galleria Alberto Sordi, p. 55

A3 **4** Metropolitan Cinema, p. 11
B3 **13** Chiesa Anglicana di Ognissanti (All Saints Anglican Church), p. 11
B5 **15** Accademia di Francia Villa Medici, p. 64
C4 **23** Galleria F. Russo, p. 64
E5 **63** Galleria dell'Accademia di San Luca, p. 64
E6 **64** Teatro Sistina, p. 71
F6 **75** Museo Nazionale delle Paste Alimentari, p. 64

⊙ HOTELS

A2 **3** Locarno, p. 81
A3 **5** Hotel de Russie, p. 82
B3 **10** Hotel Valadier, p. 83
D3 **31** Piazo, p. 83
D4 **39** Hotel d'Inghilterra, p. 82
D4 **44** Scalinata di Spagna, p. 83
D5 **45** De la Ville Inter-Continental, p. 81
D6 **50** Gregoriana Hotel, p. 81
E1 **51** Hotel Due Torre, p. 83
E5 **61** Casa Howard, p. 81
E5 **62** Dei Borgognoni, p. 81
F1 **65** Hotel Portoghesi, p. 83

MAP KEY

Major Sights	★
Metro Stop	Ⓜ Ⓜ
Shopping District	————
Stairs	ⅢⅢⅢⅢⅢⅢ
Pedestrian Street	————
Adjacent Map Boundaries	

SECTION ICONS

⊗ SIGHTS

Ⓡ RESTAURANTS

Ⓝ NIGHTLIFE

Ⓢ SHOPS

Ⓐ ARTS AND LEISURE

Ⓗ HOTELS

RESTAURANTS

MAP 3 TRIDENTE

BABINGTON'S TEA ROOMS *BREAKFAST AND BRUNCH • TEA* $$
An elegant place to get a spot o' tea, Babington's also serves pancakes and bacon until 11 PM. Tea service – formal and on the expensive side – is steeped in history at this spot where British expats like Keats and Shelley once lounged.

MAP 3 D5 Ⓡ 42 PIAZZA DI SPAGNA 23
06-67-86-027

IL BRILLO PARLANTE *AFTER HOURS • WINE BAR* $
The best place for a snack or light meal near Piazza del Popolo, this wine bar and café pours 20 wines by the glass and serves salads, pastas, and grilled meats in inviting wood-paneled rooms.

MAP 3 B3 Ⓡ 9 VIA DELLA FONTANELLA 12
06-32-43-334

Use the **MAP NUMBER, COLOR GRID COORDINATES,** and **BLACK LOCATOR NUMBER** to find the exact location of every listing in the book.

DA MARIO
Here, the menu is centered on the hearty fare, including on the freshest ingredients, photos of famous patrons testify to the authenticity of the old-time restaurant in town.

MAP 3 D5 Ⓡ 48 VIA DELLA PANETTERIA
06-67-86-027

EL TOULÀ
El Toulà is an elegant bastion of hospitality, where service is as important as food. The restaurant is a Roman institution, as are its signature dishes: *fegato alla veneziana* (sweet-and-sour liver) and baccalà mantecato (salt cod whipped with milk). Elegant dress recommended.

MAP 3 E2 Ⓡ 52 VIA DELLA LUPA 29B
06-68-73-750

IL GELATO DI SAN CRISPINO *AFTER BITES • GELATO* $
A favorite among favorites, San Crispino is so serious about gelato that you aren't allowed to eat it in a cone, as the flavor might be compromised. Sample a cup of renowned creations like balsamic vinegar, 32-year-old whiskey, Marsala wine, or honey cream.

MAP 3 D5 Ⓡ 71 VIA DELLA PANETTERIA 42
06-67-93-924

GINA *HOT SPOT • ITALIAN* $$
Posh picnics for two are prepared at this all-white eatery, complete with basket, tablecloth, glasses, panini, fruit salad, dessert, and coffee – perfect for an alfresco lunch in the nearby Borghese Gardens. Prefer to eat inside? Gina offers breakfast, lunch, and dinner (pasta, sandwiches, and salads are the standard fare) 8 AM–midnight.

MAP 3 C5 Ⓡ 28 VIA SAN SEBASTIANELLO 7A
06-67-80-251

29

v

INTRODUCTION TO
ROME

Rome is a sepia snapshot capturing thousands of years of history; its profound heritage is visible on every street corner, monument, and enduring ruin. It was once the center of the Western world and became the center of Christianity; it served as the living canvas of baroque and Renaissance masters as well as the political seat of fascist dictators; and it reveled in the dolce vita days of excess and now faces the modern-day realities of a multicultural city.

The ancient city still holds secrets of the past, as evidenced by the iconic Colosseum, the Roman Forum, and the sprawling ruins atop the Palatine Hill, where the city's fabled founders, Romulus and Remus, are said to have been born. Blossoming from the ancient roots of the Colosseo neighborhood, each of the city's other areas is a testament to the periods and influences that have shaped the Eternal City.

Vaticano holds the heart and treasures of the Catholic faith and represents Rome's transformation from a pagan city to a Christian one. The center of Rome's baroque and Renaissance periods lies in the area of Piazza Navona and the Pantheon. With Bernini's fountains, Borromini's churches, and Michelangelo's sculptures, these neighborhoods hold the collective masterpieces of some of the world's greatest artists.

Their artistic genius extends north to Tridente, where elegant fountains and piazzas punctuate the luxury saturating this center of conspicuous consumption. Once home to Goethe, Shelley, and Byron, it now hosts Gucci,

MULTICULTURAL ROME

During the days of the Roman Empire, when the invasion and capture of distant lands in turn brought the influence of foreign cultures, Rome was an early multicultural city. Today, while Romans cling to their profound heritage, their culture is again being revived and challenged by an influx of immigrants from Africa, the Middle East, India, and Eastern Europe. Rome is home to an increasing number of cultures, and their presence is adding new flavor to this provincial capital. The once all-Italian enclave around Termini Station – Esquilino – is now a multi-ethnic haven of restaurants and shops from around the world, and the exotic foods in the Vittorio market offer a welcome change from pizza and pasta. Piazza Navona, Trastevere, and many of the other city squares fill with impromptu street marts, where vendors sell everything from fake (though often convincing) Fendi and Gucci bags to handmade crafts and scarves.

Chanel, and Bulgari; these and other bastions of haute couture flank the streets leading to the Spanish Steps and on to the Trevi Fountain.

The lush life continues around the Borghese Gardens and the fashionable Via Veneto of *La Dolce Vita* fame. Here, café tables are the perfect spot for glitterati spotting. But the city shape-shifts once again, as the Via Veneto gives way to the Termini area just east. This neighborhood surrounding the main train station is Rome's multicultural hub and shows off the city's diversity in a bustling and often chaotic buzz of languages, smells, colors, and tastes.

Rome's global influences are also found in the two communities lying on either side of the snaking Tiber River. The Jewish Ghetto and Campo dei Fiori areas are a tapestry of centuries-old traditions and free-market ideals. From Europe's oldest synagogue and the kosher bakeries of the Ghetto to the vibrant open-air produce market of the Campo dei Fiori, this area offers a glimpse of everyday Roman life. Across the river, Trastevere balances its old-world charm with the international verve provided by the numerous expatriates and international students.

A visit to all of these areas, connected by ornate bridges and Vespa-filled streets, provides a complete picture of the Eternal City. Stroll the storied cobblestoned streets of each, marvel at the museums and architecture within them, appreciate the singular moment of glancing upon ruins in the middle of a metropolis, and watch the spirited Roman world pass by from streetside cafés. You'll then see why here, *la vita è bella*.

HISTORY

Rome's more than 2,000 years of history began in 753 BC when Romulus beat out his twin brother Remus for control of the seven hills of what is now Rome. From then on, Rome absorbed peoples, battled invaders, and grew into the world's first republic. Its roads led to the corners of the Western world, enveloping the whole of the Mediterranean from North Africa to Greece and beyond. Rome co-opted the cultures and treasures of each conquered land, becoming the first multicultural metropolis.

The most famous and the last of the republican rulers was Julius Caesar, whose murder on the ides of March in 44 BC sparked the beginning of the Imperial Age – a succession of enterprising emperors like Augustus and Hadrian and despotic ones like the scandalous Caligula and egocentric Nero.

Rome's empire wasn't built in a day, but its fall was swift after internal power struggles and invasions from the

A BEAUTIFUL IMAGE

For many Romans, the concept of *bella figura* (literally, beautiful image) influences just about all aspects of their lives. The phrase roughly means putting your best foot forward, and it's about looking good at all times, adding flair and fashion to just about every task, and never stepping outside social conventions. Running to the corner store? Slip on a cute dress or those Dolce slacks – never shorts and flip-flops. Bump into someone you hate? Put on a smile and kiss both cheeks in a series of boisterous "*Ciao, bella*'s." Too full to finish your plate of pasta? Never ask for a doggy bag for fear of insulting the cook. *Bella figura* may all be fake, but it sure makes for a good show.

north left it in social and political ruin until the popes filled the void in the Middle Ages. Catholicism flourished, and the Church was in charge during the artistic golden age of the baroque and Renaissance periods, when the city was re-created in sacred splendor by such masters as Michelangelo and Bernini.

Papal rule was not absolute in Italy and competed with independent city-states. Unification came in 1861 with the Kingdom of Italy led by Victor Emmanuel II, and Rome was declared the capital. But Rome would not yet know peace: the 20th century brought Benito Mussolini's fascism and devastation by German occupation and Allied bombs in World War II. In 1946, Italy returned to its republican roots and voted the monarchy out, marking the dawn of a modern country that still struggles to honor, if not recover from, its past while moving toward the future.

VESPAS

Romans call them *motorini*, motorbikes that whisk them through the city and provide the most practical solution for navigating a narrow *via* or beating the impossible parking situation. Most non-Romans call them Vespas, for the brand name that dominated in the 1950s and '60s when paparazzi clung to the two-wheeler with one hand while clicking away at stars with the other. And of course there's the famous *Roman Holiday* scene where Audrey Hepburn and Gregory Peck crash through various piazzas. Today, motorbikes swarm the streets of Rome, and their loud buzzing is a characteristic sound of the city. Pedestrians beware: They hop sidewalks, snake through traffic, and whiz through crosswalks. Tourists can rent them, but only the intrepid should dare follow in the skid marks of seasoned Roman riders. Accidents are frequent and car owners unforgiving.

PANTHEON

TRAJAN'S MARKETS

COLOSSEO

THE BEST OF
ROME

Rome was not built in a day, nor can it be seen in one. But a whirlwind tour of ancient sights right in the heart of a metropolis is an exploit that few other cities can offer. Note that this day omits the Vatican and the Sistene Chapel – the reason many come to Rome – mainly because visiting them can take a good part of the day. Instead, you'll see the best of classical Rome and sample some truly Roman experiences along the way.

1 Your first stop is **Tazza d'Oro (p. 28),** one of the city's finest cafés, to have a typical Roman stand-up breakfast of cappuccino and *cornetto*.

2 Across the way is the **Pantheon (p. 3),** an elegant ancient temple to all gods, wonderous for its perfectly shaped dome.

3 Walk over to **Trajan's Markets (p. 15),** the first of many ruins in this daylong tour. As you pass the market stalls, imagine haggling over prices for olive oil, wine, and produce 2,000 years ago.

4 To save time and money, you may want to stop at the tourist information center near the Roman Forum to find out about combined tickets to some of the sights before moving on to **Colosseo (p. 12),** the most iconic of all Roman sights.

5 Next door, the **Roman Forum/Palatine Hill (p. 13)** combination represents the heart of ancient Roman life and its birthplace. Explore the Forum, then get the best view of it from the Palatine.

⑥ Exit the Forum at the south side, and lunch will not be far away. **San Teodoro (p. 34)** is one of the few quality and convenient restaurants near the ruins.

⑦ After lunch, head to the **Campidoglio (p.11),** where the Capitoline Museums and a beautiful Michelangelo-designed piazza are located.

⑧ From there, make your way up **Via del Corso (p. 57).** Its name means "street of races," and it was used for just that in classical times. Today a main shopping corridor, it's dotted with chain stores and the occassional traditional shop.

⑨ About halfway up, turn west on Via Tomacelli to cross the Tiber River. You'll soon be at **Castel Sant'Angelo (p. 20):** The tomb and former fortress is the ideal place to see the sun set behind St. Peter's Basilica, either from the top or the small café.

⑩ Go back across the Tiber, this time on Ponte Sant'Angelo, for dinner on Via dei Banchi Nuovi, with its strip of inviting restaurants and wine bars, such as **Il Bicchiere di Mastai (p. 37).**

⑪ Finish with drinks at **Bar del Fico (p. 40).** Its pretty outdoor setting makes for the perfect, and perfectly Roman, end to the day.

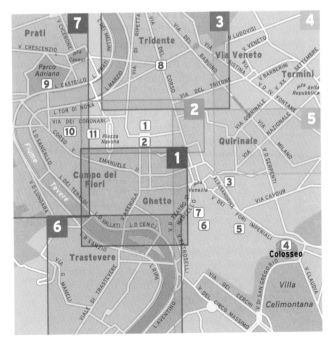

PIAZZA DI SPAGNA   HASSLER   FONTANA DI TREVI

CINEMATIC
ROME

Rome, with its monumental ruins, beautiful fountains, and bustling streets, offers a movie set unlike any other. Fellini practically invented the concept of la dolce vita here, and Audrey Hepburn's romp through Rome made many a traveler wish to follow her trail. This day gives you a glamour tour of Rome – you'll see the locations of many scenes, as well as visit the haunts of those who make them. Before you start out, you may want to get DVDs of the films as preparation and watch them on the flight over or the night before.

1 Sunglasses are required as you begin the outing with *café* or *prosecco* at **Gran Caffè Doney (p. 32)** on the Via Veneto, the street where rudderless journalist Marcello practiced the art of looking bored in Fellini's *La Dolce Vita*.

2 Stroll down Via Veneto until you hit Piazza Barberini. While visiting Rome in William Wyler's *Roman Holiday*, Ann stays at her country's embassy – the exterior "embassy" shots are actually **Palazzo Barberini (p. 64)**.

3 To the northwest, Tom Ripley juggles two women in a bar by **Piazza di Spagna (p. 8)** in *The Talented Mr. Ripley*. It's also here that Joe and Ann "accidentally" meet on the steps and start their "Roman holiday."

4 Have lunch at the **Hassler (p. 82)** hotel at the top of the steps. The service is so good that you'll feel like a movie star, and you might actually see one, too. The rooftop restaurant is a favorite perch for power brokers, heads of state, and the jet set.

⑤ Walk down to **Fontana di Trevi (p. 5),** where Sylvia takes a swirling stroll in her black-and-white evening gown in *La Dolce Vita* – don't try this stunt unless you are prepared to pay a stiff fine. Also, the three gals did their coin toss here in Jean Negulesco's *Three Coins in a Fountain*.

⑥ Eating gelato is a scene typical in so many movies set in Rome. Get one of the city's best scoops at **Il Gelato di San Crispino (p. 29).**

⑦ Make a quick detour to **Fontana delle Tartarughe (p. 3),** where Mr. Ripley kills Dickie and takes his identity.

⑧ Head over to **Bocca della Verità (p. 16).** This is where Ann and Joe face the lie detector mask in *Roman Holiday*.

⑨ Taxi over to Piazza della Repubblica for dinner at the **Hotel Exedra (p. 84),** another celebrity hot spot.

⑩ What better way to end a cinematic day than with a movie? **Warner Village Cinema Moderno (p. 73)** often shows an English-language film in one of its theaters.

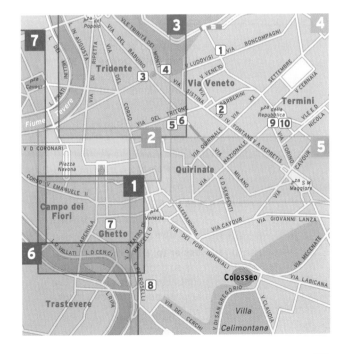

MONTE PALATINO   PIAZZA NAVONA   TEATRO ARGENTINA

MACABRE
ROME

A city with as long a history as Rome's is sure to have its share of grim and gruesome events among its glories and a number of bizarre attractions amidst its stately ruins. In fact, many sights have some grisly tale attached to them – it's just a matter of looking.

1 Start your tour at the stage of many public executions, **Piazza del Popolo (p. 10).** You can grab a quick breakfast at either of the two bars that face the piazza.

2 Walk down **Via del Corso (p. 57)** toward Trevi Fountain. Along the way, you'll pass Piazza San Lorenzo in Lucina – the grill on which St. Lawrence was killed is kept in the church of the same name.

3 Take Via Tritone east to get to **Santa Maria della Concezione (p. 65),** affectionately known as the "bone church." You'll see why: The interior decor is made up of the bones of capuchin monks.

4 Head back to **Trevi Fountain (p. 5),** and make the fabled coin toss with your back to the pool. In this position, you'll be looking at the Santi Vincenzo and Anastasio church, where the embalmed organs of numerous popes are kept. Local lore says that on Judgment Day, the innards will come flying out of the church to be reunited with the bodies, most of which are in St. Peter's.

5 Make your way down to **Monte Palatino (p. 13),** where Romulus committed fratricide and gained naming rights to the city.

⑥ Cross the Tiber into Trastevere, and stop by the church of **Santa Cecilia (p. 18),** where Cecilia faced her martyrdom. The church's artwork illustrates the story.

⑦ Stop for a lunch at **Panattoni (p. 36),** which is also known as "L'Obitorio" (the morgue) for the marble slabs used to make the pizza here.

⑧ Take the tram from Viale Trastevere to the end of the line, Largo Argentina, to visit **Area Sacra dell'Argentina (p. 2),** where Julius Caesar was stabbed to death.

⑨ Walk over to **Piazza Navona (p. 4)** and the church, Sant'Agnese. Agnes's martyrdom included surviving boiling oil and flames before succumbing to being beheaded.

⑩ Nearby, in **Campo dei Fiori (p. 2),** Giordano Bruno, considered a heretic by the church, was burned at the stake in 1600. Get dinner at one of the many restaurants around the square and on its side streets.

⑪ End your day back at Largo Argentina with a play at **Teatro Argentina (p. 71).** With a bit of luck, there will be a good tragedy showing!

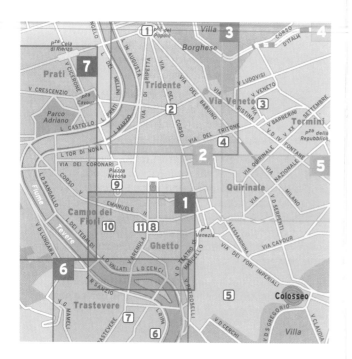

GHETTO/ CAMPO DEI FIORI

Rome may have a strong connection to Christianity, but it's also home to Europe's oldest Jewish community. Centuries of community and faith have shaped the character-filled neighborhood of the Ghetto. The narrow streets are lined with buildings stretching seven stories high, a reminder that Jews were forced to build tenements upward when anti-Semitic popes confined them to this area. After the walls separating the Ghetto from the rest of Rome were torn down and after the World War II terror of Nazi deportations, the neighborhood remains at once a close community and an inviting place to explore. Surrounding the riverside synagogue are piazzas boasting excellent restaurants, random ancient ruins, and delicate fountains.

The boutique feel of the Ghetto bursts into a splash of colors and sounds in Campo dei Fiori. By day, its long piazza is a harvest-filled market full of Italians shopping for their next meal. By night, the square fills with young revelers headed for the many pubs and restaurants. It can make for sensory overload, but Piazza Farnese's peaceful fountains, ivy-lined Via Giulia, and quaint back streets offer a calmer experience.

MAP 1 GHETTO/CAMPO DEI FIORI

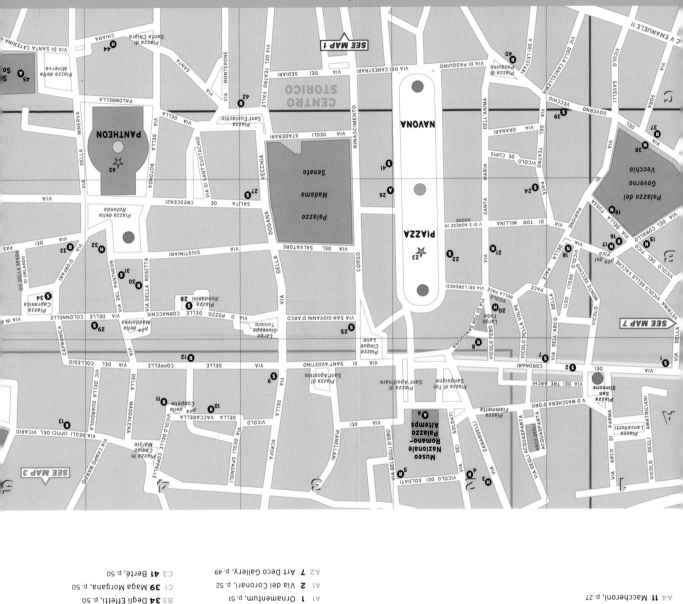

MAP 2 PIAZZA NAVONA/PANTHEON

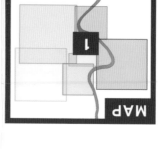

PIAZZA NAVONA/ PANTHEON

Once the open studio of baroque and Renaissance masters, vibrant Piazza Navona holds one of Rome's most splendid fountains. The sound of rushing water around Bernini's Four Rivers fountain competes with the din of tourists, Italians, and vendors filling both the square and the bistro tables surrounding it. Away from this bubbling atmosphere, in the tranquil side streets branching out from the piazza, you'll discover quaint cafés, unique stores, and original galleries. The entire area becomes a masterpiece at sunset, when a surreal golden light falls on faded-ochre buildings and the lights of the fountain reflect in the pools.

Across the Corso Rinascimento, the Pantheon neighborhood balances a number of contrasts. Tour groups headed to the main attraction – the ancient architectural wonder the area is named for – mix with business-suited politicos headed for the Italian senate and other government offices nearby; restaurants catering to vacationers neighbor some of Rome's most exceptional dining options; and intimate piazzas that tuck away curious shops are nestled among bustling squares that buzz from Rome's best coffee.

MAGRIPPALF·COSTERTIVM·FEC

1

B6 **16** Chiesa del Gesù, p. 3
C2 **21** ✱ Campo dei Fiori, p. 2
C4 **28** Area Sacra dell'Argentina and the Cat Sanctuary, p. 2
D5 **34** Fontana delle Tartarughe, p. 3
F6 **40** Teatro di Marcello, p. 3

● RESTAURANTS

B1 **8** Al Bric, p. 24
B3 **12** Acqua Negra, p. 24
B4 **14** Vecchia Locanda, p. 25
C1 **17** Caffè Farnese, p. 24
C1 **19** Il Forno di Campo dei Fiori, p. 25
C1 **20** Vineria, p. 26
C2 **24** Filetti di Baccalà, p. 24
D3 **32** Crudo, p. 24
D4 **33** Zì Fenizia, p. 26
E4 **35** Piperno, p. 25
E5 **37** Da Giggetto, p. 24

● NIGHTLIFE

A4 **3** Supper Club, p. 40
C1 **18** Taverna del Campo, p. 40

● SHOPS

A5 **4** Amore e Psiche, p. 48
A6 **5** Confetteria Moriondo e Gariglio, p. 48
B1 **6** Rachele, p. 49
B1 **7** Mondello Ottica, p. 48
B4 **15** Antica Erboristeria, p. 48
C2 **22** Pinko, p. 48
C2 **25** Best Seller, p. 48
C4 **26** Spazio Sette, p. 49
C6 **30** Rinascita, p. 49
E5 **36** Leone Limentani, p. 48

● ARTS AND LEISURE

A1 **1** Museo Barracco di Scultura Antica, p. 62
A2 **2** Palazzo Braschi Museo di Roma, p. 62
B2 **9** Romarent, p. 76
B2 **10** Associazione Culturale l'Attico, p. 62
C4 **27** Teatro Argentina, p. 71
C5 **29** Museo Nazionale Romano – Crypta Balbi, p. 62
D1 **31** Galleria Spada, p. 62
E6 **38** Sala Baldini, p. 71
F5 **39** Museo Ebraico di Roma, p. 62

● HOTELS

B2 **11** Albergo del Sole al Biscione, p. 80
B3 **13** Hotel Tiziano, p. 80
C2 **23** Teatro di Pompeo, p. 80

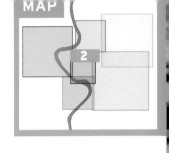

MAP 2

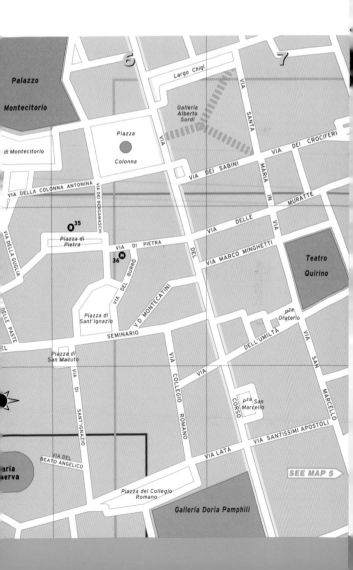

TRIDENTE

Tridente is named for the trio of avenues fanning out from Piazza del Popolo, but it's better known for its glitz and unabashed consumption. Rome's most luxurious shops are nestled here, including haute couture houses like Valentino and Dior, top-shelf jewelers like Bulgari and Buccellati, and refined individual stores purveying handmade silks, leather, or one-of-a-kind treasures.

Via Condotti is the Rodeo Drive of Rome, hosting a constant flow of well-heeled Romans and tourists doing their share to boost the Italian economy. Designer shops line this and other streets leading away from the postcard-perfect Spanish Steps, but there are also places for art and antiques lovers to splurge in ornate stores and quiet galleries.

More than just a shopper's mecca, Tridente has history and beauty to rival that of other areas of Rome. The lush and serene Villa Borghese lies a world away from the commercial bustle below; Trevi Fountain, with its breathtaking proportions and intricate sculptures often obscured by coin-tossing visitors, is a masterpiece in water and stone; and the whole area has the distinction of being the one-time home of such greats as Byron, Keats, Shelley, and Bernini.

MAP 3 TRIDENTE

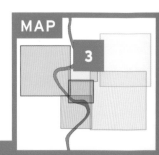

MAP

3

VIA VENETO/TERMINI

The 1960 Fellini classic, *La Dolce Vita,* made Via Veneto an international symbol of the "sweet life," one filled with beautiful people leading glamorous lives in the café catwalks of Rome. Although the glitterati and the paparazzi have long abandoned Via Veneto as their favored haunt, the area remains a bastion of elegance and class. Five-star hotels, wicker bistro chairs, and refined Roman stores line the famous avenue as it snakes from the green oasis of Villa Borghese down to Piazza Barberini.

The subdued beauty of this area ranges from the superb collections inside the Galleria Borghese and Palazzo Barberini to the breathtaking view from the Palazzo del Quirinale. Heading east, the sweet life gives way to a faster-paced one. Round the fountain in Piazza della Repubblica, and you enter a world of chaotic commuters heading to and from Termini station, Rome's transportation hub. Around the station, the city takes on an international flair thanks to the immigrant residents. They bring their vibrant cultures and cuisine to the tiny restaurants and sprawling markets and make this area a colorful addition to the often-homogenous Rome.

MAP 4 VIA VENETO/TERMINI

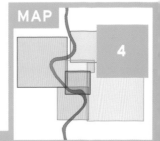

MAP 4

COLOSSEO

The circular ruins of the Colosseum and the skeletal Roman Forum are the center of the ancient city. These are the proud icons of Rome's profound history, and each of the remains surrounding these sites paints a vivid picture of life in the time of Caesar. The mini-city atop the Palatine Hill allows a vivid glance into early community life, the mall-like structure of Trajan's Markets hint at the commercial zeal, the Domus Aurea gives a peek at the excesses of Imperial Rome, and the oblong field of Circus Maximus reveals a bit of the old-school entertainment.

Beyond the shadow of the ancient city, Santa Maria Maggiore, San Giovanni in Laterano, and San Clemente are among the city's most important Catholic churches. The surrounding communities are all up-and-coming neighborhoods in this area that once had little else to offer than a history lesson. Monti, just behind Trajan's Forum, is filled with eclectic shops and ethnic restaurants. Above the Colosseum, Celio, with its park-like setting and interesting new bars, is the perfect place to ponder all of the wonders of the ancient world.

MAP 5 COLOSSEO

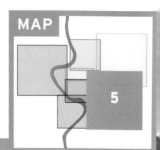

MAP

5

TRASTEVERE

The clotheslines canopying the narrow streets and the flowers cascading from tiny balconies are only part of what makes Trastevere one of Rome's most colorful and enchanting neighborhoods. Historically home to foreigners – the likes of Cleopatra and Napoleon's mother – it is a community of artistic expatriates, globally minded locals, and young students from the United States. By night, the many bars, restaurants, and lively piazzas come to life in a multilingual buzz, creating a small-town feel with a worldly slant. The piazza of Santa Maria in Trastevere is the heart of the neighborhood, and the eponymous basilica is the soul. Adorned in gilded mosaics, the basilica is believed to be Rome's oldest place of worship dedicated to the Virgin Mary.

Across the river is the Aventino area, which takes its name from the hill that was said to belong to Remus, Romulus's rival twin. Don't miss the Piazza dei Cavalieri di Malta, where a keyhole gives a miniature view of St. Peter's Basilica.

MAP 6 TRASTEVERE

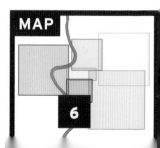

MAP

6

VATICANO

Although Vatican City is a sovereign state, it's one of Rome's most important areas. Its citizens only number into the hundreds, but millions of visitors from around the world come here every day to see the many treasures held within the Vatican walls. St. Peter's Basilica and Square, the Sistine Chapel, and the masterpiece-filled rooms in the Vatican Museums hold an incredible wealth of sacred and secular art and history.

Where the Vatican's postal code and Swiss guard boundaries end, the rest of Vaticano can seem like a de facto extension of the pope-centered world. Nuns, priests, and pilgrims mix with everyday tourists. Shops and newspaper stands sell religious items and T-shirts bearing the pope's likeness. The secular side of Vaticano offers bountiful shopping streets like Cola di Rienzo and interesting dining options around Piazza Cavour. Nearby, the riverside fortress of Castel Sant'Angelo, the area's other major sight, is connected to the Vatican via underground tunnels once used by under-siege popes seeking refuge. Its beautiful bridge, lined with vendors, leads across the river to an elbow of land that hints at the adjacent Piazza Navona area with restaurant streets like Via dei Banchi Nuovi.

MAP 7 VATICANO

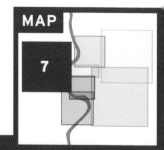

MAP

7

★ SIGHTS

MAP 1 | **GHETTO/CAMPO DEI FIORI**

CAMPO DEI FIORI

Bustling food market by day and alfresco bar scene by night, this piazza buzzes from early morning until the wee hours. The name, field of flowers, refers not to today's flower vendors but hearkens back to bucolic days in ancient times. Campo dei Fiori was the site of races, tournaments, and executions – all public entertainment before the market moved here from Piazza Navona in 1869.

The bronze statue in the center is ex-Dominican philosopher Giordano Bruno, burned the stake here at in 1600 for his rebellious notions. Protestors and rabble-rousers congregate around the statue periodically to press their causes, but today Bruno serves mostly as a rendezvous point. Nearby, innkeeper Vanozza's 15th-century trysts with future Pope Alexander VI produced, among others, the infamous Lucrezia and Cesare Borgia. (Lucrezia went on to be married a number of times – with some of her husbands meeting suspicious ends – while brother Cesare became Machiavelli's model for *The Prince*.) Today, Romans jostle past Vanozza's door at no. 13 and into the corner *forno*, one of Rome's most famous bakeries specializing in bread and pizza.

Many of Rome's chefs do their buying at the market here, in one of Rome's few squares not anchored by a church. Arrive in the morning in time to see locals buying the makings for lunch and dinner. If you want to have a picnic, the square is ideal for picking up all the fixings, as cheese, salami, and wine shops all are right here. The market disappears around lunchtime, the detritus is cleared, and at night the demimonde spills out onto the piazza in Rome's most notorious and noisy outdoor drinking scene. For better dining, try the spots on the side streets off the piazza.

 C2✪21 PIAZZA CAMPO DEI FIORI
MARKET HOURS: MON.-SAT. 7 AM-1 PM

AREA SACRA DELL'ARGENTINA AND THE CAT SANCTUARY

This large square once had temples dedicated to four early Roman gods like Feronia and Fortuna, and Caesar was killed just steps away from them. Now the domain of hundreds of abandoned cats, a sanctuary below street level is tended by feline-friendly volunteers. Open by appointment only.

 C4✪28 LARGO DI TORRE ARGENTINA
06-68-72-133

CAMPO
DEI FIORI   PANTHEON

CHIESA DEL GESÙ

Il Gesù's austere travertine facade would influence church design for a century after its completion in 1584. But it belies the sumptuous interior that boasts frescoes by Il Baciccia and the ornate, silver- and gold-heavy Chapel of St. Ignatius Loyola.

 B6✪16 PIAZZA DEL GESÙ
06-69-70-01

FONTANA DELLE TARTARUGHE

Giacomo della Porta, the architect who designed the facade of Il Gesù, turns playful here with a design from the same period that incorporates boys holding water-spewing dolphins. Bernini is thought to have added the namesake turtles in a 1658 restoration.

MAP 1 D5✪34 PIAZZA MATTEI

TEATRO DI MARCELLO

Begun by Julius Caesar and completed by Augustus in AD 13 in memory of his nephew, this theater once seated 15,000 spectators. You can't go inside – apartments were built in the ruins – but you can still appreciate its grand arches and columns.

MAP 1 F6✪40 VIA DEL TEATRO DI MARCELLO

MAP 2 PIAZZA NAVONA/PANTHEON

PANTHEON

The best-preserved building from imperial Rome, the Pantheon started out as a temple to honor all gods (earning its name) built in 27 BC by Agrippa. Emperor Hadrian later revised its design (AD 118–125) significantly with an engineering feat that would baffle mankind for centuries afterward. Imagine the dome as the cap of a

PIAZZA NAVONA

FONTANA
DI TREVI

perfect sphere (its diameter equals its height). Its construction mystified even expert Renaissance and modern architects: Why were the walls, the dome's only support, not crushed under its tremendous weight? The secret was lost in Rome's decline.

Subsequently abandoned for about 200 years, the building was given to the pope in 608, a gift that somewhat saved the temple by converting it to a church to Mary and the Martyrs. However, papal plundering of its own property began swiftly: in 663 its brilliant gilded roof was stripped, to be re-covered in 735 in lead. In 1625, Pope Urban VIII took the bronze portico to construct 80 cannons for Castel Sant'Angelo and removed some columns to use for St. Peter's. (*"Quod non fecerunt barbari, fecerunt Barberini"* – "what the barbarians didn't do, Barberini did.")

Despite these indignities, the Pantheon remains a majestic building. Its only sources of light come from above and from the open door. The oculus of the dome, the eye toward heaven, lets in light as well as rain or snow – an exalting experience in any weather. Renaissance artist Raphael's tomb lies within, in the company of kings, such as Vittorio Emanuele II, unified Italy's first.

For maximum dramatic effect, approach the Pantheon from the north. As it looms into view, the harmonious, imposing, and austere form will be striking.

 MAP 2 C4 **43** PIAZZA DELLA ROTONDA 06-68-30-02-30
HOURS: MON.-SAT. 8:30 AM-7:30 PM, SUN. 9 AM-6 PM, HOLIDAYS
9 AM-1 PM

PIAZZA NAVONA

Piazza Navona is the ideal spot to linger in conversation at coffee bars and to browse in quality shops and art galleries, and it has been a social scene in Rome for more than 2,000 years. During the times of Caesar and Augustus, the plaza hosted sporting matches. Later, in AD 86, Emperor Domitian built a stadium that could hold 30,000 spectators. Today the spectators are seated in outdoor cafés as they admire the dramatic baroque fountains and watch the landscape of Romans, tourists, lovers, artists, fortunetellers, and souvenir vendors that are drawn to this large, grand square.

Medieval houses, Renaissance palaces, and baroque churches fuse together to provide a beautiful backdrop for the energy and movement within the square's racetrack form. The centerpiece is the Fontana dei Fiumi, Gian Lorenzo Bernini's 1651 fountain of the four main rivers of the then-known world: Nile, Ganges, Danube, and Plata. Bernini himself sculpted the horse and lion, leaving talented assistants to complete most of his design. The obelisk on top is a 1st-century Roman copy of an Egyptian obelisk.

To the west of the fountain, Sant'Agnese in Agone church — built by rival architect Francesco Borromini — stands on the spot of a 4th-century brothel where the Christian teen Agnes was stripped and thrown after refusing to marry a pagan of high rank. Her hair then miraculously grew to cover her.

At the south end, exit toward Via del Governo Vecchio and Piazza di Pasquino, where at no. 104 is the 3rd-century BC bust of Pasquino, one of a handful of Rome's *statue parlante* (talking statues), where passing citizens posted notes of gossip, news, and predictions — an ancient chat room still in use today.

 MAP 2 B2 ❷23 PIAZZA NAVONA

MAP 3 | TRIDENTE

FONTANA DI TREVI

Rome is a city of fountains, and Trevi is the fountain of fountains. You can sense its exuberance and excitement even before you find it: The small piazza surrounding the fountain magnifies the force of the water and carries the sound out into the nearby streets. And then you see the fountain: Nicola Salvi's extravagant

APPIA ANTICA EXCURSION

The most famous of the consular roads that led into and out of ancient Rome, the Appia Antica — today protected as a regional park — makes for an idyllic outing that takes you beyond the city. It offers up antiquities, subterranean catacombs, exclusive villas hidden behind walls, and pastoral vistas and is an ideal half- or full-day excursion to explore on foot or by bike. Among the many fascinating sights located here, these are the highlights.

PORTA SAN SEBASTIANO
Located at the beginning of Appia Antica, St. Sebastian's Gate is an opening in the Aurelian wall that helped protect Rome from invading enemies. Just inside is the **Museo delle Mura (p. 70),** worth a visit to climb atop the ancient wall.

QUO VADIS
According to tradition, as St. Peter was fleeing persecution under Nero, a vision of Christ appeared to him at the site of this church and said, *"Quo vadis?"* (where are you going?). On the floor inside are footprints imbedded in marble, said to have been left by Christ, although archeologists say that this was a pagan sign that meant "have a good trip."

CATACOMBE DI SAN CALLISTO/ CATACOMBE DI SAN SEBASTIANO
In the 5th century BC, a religious mandate prohibited burials inside the city walls; as a result Romans interred the dead in underground cemeteries, or catacombs. More than 200 miles of tombs lie beneath Appia Antica, but Christian burial sites like the Catacombs of San Callisto and San Sebastiano are the most popular with visitors.

scene, completed in 1762, depicts Oceanus as the central deity amidst his cavorting court of giant sea horses and conch-blowing tritons.

The central section represents Fame, while side niches tell other stories. In one, Salubriety as a virgin reveals to soldiers the source of the spring that feeds into the fountain. In another scene, Agrippa approves the design for the aqueduct that brought the spring's water to Rome in 19 BC. The pool that spreads out in front of the fountain represents the sea. The name Trevi probably refers

The Catacombs of San Callisto are the oldest and best preserved in the city. Sixteen popes and 50 martyrs are buried here, with frescoes that date to the 2nd and 3rd centuries AD. A historic pilgrimage site as the place where St. Sebastian is buried, the San Sebastiano Catacombs played an important role in expanding the popularity of these underground cemeteries, but they are more damaged as a result of the easy access.

MILE MARKER THREE
At this point, the brick or asphalt road gives way to the ancient basalt stones. In some parts, you can still see ancient wagon tracks. This is also where a half-day trip would end, but if you continue on, the sights include the tomb of a priestess to the goddess Isis that dates from the 1st century AD and the remains of an ancient bath, aqueducts, and the Villa dei Quintilli, the largest suburban villa of its time.

To get to the Appia Antica, take a taxi to Porto San Sebastiano. (A bus ride is also possible for the unhurried.) The best day to visit is Sunday, when the road is blocked to most car traffic. You'll definitely want to stop by the park office (Via Appia Antica 58/60, 06-51-35-316; hours: daily 9:30 AM–5:30 PM, until 4:30 PM in winter) for brochures and maps or to rent a bike. For sustenance, L'Escargot (Via Appia Antica 46, 06-51-36-791; closed Mon.) is located toward the beginning of the road. This French restaurant is a relic in its own right as a survivor of the 1960s when it was a chic spot for the dolce vita crowd.

to the fountain's location at the junction of three roads, or *tre vie*.

The fountain's beauty and history, not to mention Anita Ekberg's unforgettable frolic through it in *La Dolce Vita*, have made Trevi a must-see on many travelers' itineraries. The small square is often crowded, so consider seeing the fountain during mealtimes, very early in the morning, or at night. And before re-enacting Ekberg's dip in the fountain, think about the stiff fine from the police – even Fellini used a set. Instead, try the famous coin toss: With your back to the fountain, throw a coin into it over your left shoulder. If you do this, legend has it, you will ensure your future return to Rome.

MAP 3 **F5✪73** PIAZZA DI TREVI

PIAZZA DI SPAGNA

Beautiful Piazza di Spagna makes for one of the greatest urban stage sets: The Spanish Steps spill elegantly down into the plaza, with the twin towers of the French Trinità dei Monti church rising above. The piazza is also located in the midst of such famous shopping streets as Via Condotti and Via Babuino, adding well-heeled shoppers to the throngs of tourists seeking a photo-op.

Built between 1723 and 1726, the Francesco de Sanctis-designed staircase takes its name from the Spanish Embassy to the Vatican, located near the base of the steps. In the early 1800s, foreigners sought lodging near the steps while waiting for their goods to clear customs, attracting a sizeable British community that included romantics like Keats and Shelley.

A visit here calls for a grand-entrance sweep down the stairs from the top or a hardy hike up from the bottom. Whichever approach you choose, take time to perch on a step for international people-watching. (You'll be glad for the respite: Rome has a noticeable lack of outdoor benches.) Next to the steps is the Keats–Shelly house (Piazza di Spagna 26), which includes the apartment where Keats died of tuberculosis in 1821 and is now a museum.

The steps are at their most glorious – and crowded – in late spring when azaleas cascade down the stone staircases. Huge pots of purple, pink, red, and salmon blossoms adorn the flights and terraces in a blaze of color that can be seen from blocks away. Off on the side streets purple wisteria vines gently twine around walls and gates.

MAP 3 **C5✪29** PIAZZA DI SPAGNA

VILLA BORGHESE

Villa Borghese is Rome's most popular park. An urban oasis like London's Hyde Park and New York City's Central Park, it draws flocks of city dwellers searching for fresh air and diversion. Intimate gardens give way to small hills and valleys in an odd mix of formal and unkempt that, especially on weekends, offers a rare

PIAZZA DI SPAGNA VILLA BORGHESE

glimpse of Roman family life, when all are out taking their *passagiata* (stroll), biking, or walking dogs.

Cardinal Scipione Borghese Caffarelli, a 17th-century hedonist and beloved nephew of Pope Paul V, began the Villa Borghese in 1608 as a Renaissance garden surrounded by a grove of trees, a "garden of perspective" to show off the antique art collection, and a park that was rustic and natural. Vineyards, exotic plants, and Mediterranean fruit trees were later included by Jacob More, an 18th-century painter, and others to evoke a more natural style in vogue with the British at that time. Eventually the property was purchased by Italy in 1901 and given to Rome in 1903.

Modern-day Romans use the expansive grounds for all manner of activities. In 2003, the Globe Theatre was constructed after the replica in London, and now hosts readings and plays. Piazza di Siena has an amphitheater that hosts horse races and other events. You can go up in a balloon, rent a bicycle (or other wheeled contraptions), ride horses in a ring, see a movie in the tiny cinema, or picnic by a lake. There's also Galleria Borghese, one of the park's major attractions. The sumptuous displays include some of the best works of Bernini, Caravaggio, Raphael, Rubens, and others, as well as Roman antiquities.

MAP 3 B6 ⊕16   MAIN ENTRANCE AT PIAZZALE BRASILE
HOURS: SUNRISE-SUNSET (RESERVATIONS REQUIRED FOR GALLERIA BORGHESE)

ARA PACIS

The Altar of Peace, with its intricate friezes, was dedicated in 9 BC to celebrate Augustus's victories in Gaul and Spain. This monument is scheduled to reopen in 2006 after the controversial construction of a Richard Meier–designed museum around it.

MAP 3 C2 ⊕19   VIA DI RIPETTA
06-67-10-38-19

MAUSOLEO DI AUGUSTO

The emperor of Rome's Golden Age and his family were buried in this circular, but now neglected and trash-spotted, monument. It's hard to believe that inside lie the likes of Augustus, Livia, Agrippa, and Tiberius. The tomb can be visited during weekend mornings, but phone ahead.

 C2✪20 PIAZZA AUGUSTO IMPERATORE
06-67-10-38-19

PIAZZA DEL POPOLO

Giuseppe Valadier designed this enormous, busy piazza in 1811, completed in 1824. Once the stage for fairs, sporting matches, and executions, this square also holds Rome's second-oldest obelisk, which was built by Ramses II in 1200 BC and brought to Rome by Augustus. Don't miss the splendid paintings by Caravaggio and Pinturrichio in Santa Maria del Popolo, one of the churches on the square.

 A2✪1 PIAZZA DEL POPOLO

 VIA VENETO/TERMINI

FONTANA DELL'ACQUA FELICE

This 1587 fountain features a trio of niches that shelter water-themed biblical sculptures. The middle statue of Moses, by Leonardo Sormani and Prospero Bresciano, suffers from an unfavorable comparison to Michelangelo's work in San Pietro in Vincoli.

 D3✪20 PIAZZA SAN BERNARDO

PIAZZA DELLA REPUBBLICA (PIAZZA ESEDRA)

The playful scene of four bronze Naiads cavorting with sea creatures in this piazza's centerpiece fountain (Fontana delle Naiadi) created a scandal when unveiled in 1901. The only recent scandal is the bad restoration done in 2000 that is now peeling like a bad sunburn.

MAP 4 D3✪24 PIAZZA DELLA REPUBBLICA

QUATTRO FONTANE

Representing the Tiber, Arno, Juno, and Diana, four baroque fountains (1588-1593), each in a corner niche, mark this intersection. The sculptures were partially restored, but air pollution damage could not be removed on some of the most intricate parts.

MAP 4 E2✪30 VIA DELLE QUATTRO FONTANE AT VIA DEL QUIRINALE

SANTA MARIA MAGGIORE

One of four great pilgrimage churches in the city, St. Mary Major, was built on the site of a miraculous snowfall on August 5, AD

CAMPIDOGLIO

QUATTRO FONTANE

356. Combining Romanesque, baroque, and other styles, the design incorporates a ceiling gilded with the first gold brought from the New World and breathtaking medieval mosaics.

  PIAZZA DI SANTA MARIA MAGGIORE
06-48-81-094 OR 06-48-31-95

SANT'ANDREA AL QUIRINALE

Commissioned in 1654, this unusual church features a clever Bernini-designed oval floor plan. Don't miss the altar of bronze and lapis lazuli in the main chapel.

   VIA DEL QUIRINALE 29
06-48-90-31-87

MAP 5 | COLOSSEO

CAMPIDOGLIO/MUSEI CAPITOLINI

Campidoglio (Capitoline Hill) was the most important of Rome's seven hills: It is the headquarters of civic government – and has been since the city was founded. The grand and harmonious Piazza del Campidoglio, designed by Michelangelo, unites buildings dedicated to art and to politics (although politics is scheduled to give way to art as future development plans include relocating the mayor's office to enlarge the museum complex).

Inaugurated in BC 509 by King Tarquin, the hill was the site of temples to Jupiter (the symbolic father of the city), Minerva (the goddess of wisdom), and Juno Monete (guardian goddess of the city's treasures). Two millennia later, in 1537, Pope Paul III commissioned Michelangelo to design the Piazza del Campidoglio as a matter of civic pride since the area had become a mess of goats and mud.

The *cordonata*, a grand ramp, leads up to the square.

 COLOSSEO   FORO ROMANO

At the center is the bronze sculpture of Marcus Aurelius astride his horse, and Palazzo Senatorio (city hall), built by Giacomo della Porta and Girolamo Rainaldi after a Michelangelo design, is situated above a statue of Athena and a fountain of the Tiber River god.

Palazzo dei Conservatori and Palazzo Nuovo form the Musei Capitolini (Capitoline Museums). Dating from 1568 and 1655, respectively, they are the world's oldest public museums, thanks in part to donations from art patron Pope Sixtus who had acquired vast collections of classical sculpture. The most moving is the *Dying Gaul,* dignified as his young life slips away. Ideal female beauty can be found in several versions of Venus and Cleopatra. Ruling the courtyard, the colossal head and pointing hand are the most significant bits that remain of the statue of Constantine. In other media, the Pinacoteca (picture gallery) paintings include Caravaggio's *La Buona Ventura* and Rubens's *Romulus and Remus.* Also among the collections is the 5th-century BC bronze sculpture of the she-wolf that suckled twins Romulus and Remus – a symbol of the city.

MAP 5 C1 ⊕22   PIAZZA DEL CAMPIDOGLIO 06-39-96-78-00 OR 06-67-10-20-71
MUSEUM HOURS: TUES.-SUN. 9 AM-8 PM

COLOSSEO

Colosseo (Colosseum) is the symbol of Eternal Rome, as iconic to the city as the Empire State Building is to New York and the Eiffel Tower is to Paris. A tribute to its glory and ingenuity, as well as a reminder of its excesses and cruelty, Colosseo embodies ancient Rome.

Construction on Colosseo began in AD 72 at the behest of Emperor Vespasian and was inaugurated by Titus in AD 80 with games that lasted 100 days. During medieval times, the amphitheater became known popularly as the

"Colosseum," for the colossal gilded bronze statue of Nero that once stood in the structure.

Surrounded on the outside by 80 arches of travertine, Colosseo could hold about 50,000 spectators for its "sporting events." The design made use of engineering advances of the time such as the Roman arch. Its *vomitoria*, which were cleverly designed exit stairways, could disgorge the entire crowd in a matter of minutes after the performance was over (this model influenced modern entertainment arenas). The elevator shafts, still visible from above, were used to introduce gladiators, animals, or elaborate stage sets that could pop up at any time to change the scene and thrill or delight the audience.

More than its engineering feats, the Colosseum is better known today for the spectacles that were held within it. Gladiators fought wild animals and each other for the entertainment of all. During these combat exhibitions, a winner was declared only after his opponent had been slaughtered. Human gladiator fights ended in AD 404, and Romans tired of all their grisly games around the 6th century. In 1312, Colosseo became the property of the Senate and People of Rome, but it was still looted for its metal supports and massive marble and stone blocks that were recycled in churches and palaces. Pope Benedict XIV ebbed the marble flow when he consecrated the remains as a church in the 18th century; today the Pope visits its Stations of the Cross as part of Easter ceremonies.

Today the Colosseum is Rome's primary attraction, drawing long lines of visitors. The city occasionally allows part of it to be used for special events, which are rare and always very tame by ancient standards.

 PIAZZA DEL COLOSSEO 06-39-96-77-00 OR 06-70-05-469 HOURS: DAILY 8:30 AM-6:15 PM (SPRING); DAILY 9 AM-3:30 PM (WINTER)

FORO ROMANO/MONTE PALATINO

As the center of the Empire, the Foro Romano (Roman Forum) was the combined Wall Street and Washington, DC, of its day — the financial, political, and power center of the known world. Unlike many other Roman monuments, the Forum was not built from one imperial decree, but rather, it evolved. As agricultural land evolved into food markets, other commerce moved in, along with temples, administrative government offices, courts of law, and taverns. Eventually the major power

COMMEMORATIVE PLAQUES

It's one thing to defeat Carthigians, Gauls, and Persians, but it's quite another to get credit for it. Ancient Romans solved this problem by dedicating marble plaques to themselves. Traces of these can still be seen along the **Appia Antica (p. 6),** at the **Forum (p. 13),** and in the ancient harbor town of Ostia Antica. The plaque tradition outlived the Empire, and they are found throughout the city. They mark the houses where John Keats died (Piazza di Spagna 26), Samuel Morse deciphered code (Via Prefetti 17), Goethe was inspired (Via del Corso 18), and countless musicians, philosophers, and poets lived. Many commemorate victims of World War II, and Piazza San Paolo contains a large plaque dedicated to the resistance. Knowledge of Latin or Italian is useful for reading these mementos to the past and learning who slept where.

center squeezed out the small market life, but the forum remained the center of social and political dealings in republican Rome.

Unfortunately, after the decline of the Roman Empire, the forum buildings were pillaged for materials until it became a dump and a pasture for grazing animals. Its remains were submerged except for the tops of a few columns and the victory arches of Septimius Severus and Titus. Today, Via Sacra, the main path through the site, still has basalt stones from the original roads with traces of wagon tracks. Antonius's temple to his deceased wife, Faustina, is among the best preserved ruins because a church had been built above it.

A visit to the Forum takes at least an hour. The best approach is to have a detailed map (the ticket office sells maps and booklets). Skip the confusing audio guide, which lacks good orientation points and offers no information about many of the buildings.

Afterward, don't miss Monte Palatino (Palatine Hill), where legend says Romulus founded Rome in 753 BC. It's worth the climb to see where the rich and powerful once lived — it still has traces of the villas of Augustus and his wife, Livia. The view from Palatino encompasses Aventine Hill and Circus Maximus, as well as the Forum. There's also the great Museo

Palatino that illustrates some of the history of this famous hill.

MAP 5 C2 ✪24   FORO ROMANO: VIA DEI FORI IMPERIALI 06-39-96-77-00
HOURS: DAILY 9 AM-4:30 PM (WINTER); DAILY 9 AM-7:30 PM
(SUMMER)

MAP 5 D2 ✪24   MONTE PALATINO: VIA DI SAN GREGORIO 20 • 06-39-96-77-00
HOURS: DAILY 9 AM-4:30 PM (WINTER); DAILY 9 AM-7:30 PM
(SUMMER)

MERCATI DI TRAIANO

Foro di Traiano (Trajan's Forum) was the grandest of all Roman forums. It had the Basilica Ulpia, which featured Rome's tallest and most extravagant columns, Greek and Latin libraries, and other civic buildings that made it a hub of daily life in ancient Rome. Adding to the bustle, Mercati di Traiano (Trajan's Markets), located next to the forum, were a multilevel shopping center that was abuzz with vendors selling oil, fish, or produce in the 150 stalls. Here, residents also gathered at *tabernae* – ancient Rome's version of wine bars.

Apollodorus of Damascus designed Emperor Trajan's grandiose forum, which was constructed in AD 107 and decorated with the finest colored marble from across the Empire (look for hues in column and pavement fragments). Today, the best-preserved parts of this area are the markets; they survived in part because of their functional purpose and because they lacked political or religious significance. The exedra, a gigantic curved wall with seating underneath, accommodated both private and public meetings. Thanks to a restoration, you can now walk around the market stalls that remain a wonder of ancient architecture.

 MAP 5 B2 ✪11   VIA IV NOVEMBRE 94 • 06-69-78-05-32
HOURS: TUES.-SUN. 9 AM-6 PM

SAN CLEMENTE

San Clemente is the ideal way to travel vertically through time. Start in the late Middle Ages, then go back to early Middle Ages, and finish in antiquity.

Built over earlier churches, the current San Clemente was built in 1108 and incorporates features of the 4th-century and 2nd-century structures that came before it. The marble panels near the altar came from the second incarnation of the church and are painted with doves, fish, and vines – symbols of the early Christian church. St. Clement is buried in a sunken tomb at the front of the altar. Also on this first level are the 15th-century frescoes on the left wall, which tell the story of

ARCO DI CONSTANTINO   FORUM BOARIUM

St. Catherine of Alexandria, and a colorful 12th-century mosaic depicting biblical scenes.

Below the current church lies the second of the three buildings. This 4th-century level is fairly well preserved, with frescoes that recount the legend of St. Clement, Italy's fourth pope, who was exiled to Crimea by Emperor Trajan.

Underneath the 4th-century ruins is yet another layer of history, a 2nd-century structure that encloses a shrine to the cult of Mithra. This monotheistic religion predated Christianity and probably originated near Persia. These ruins show a space in which secret rituals and celebratory banquets were held.

 D4 ✪40   VIA DI SAN GIOVANNI IN LATERANO 06-70-45-10-18 HOURS: MON.-SAT. 9 AM-12:30 PM, 3-6 PM; SUN. 10 AM-12:30 PM, 3-6 PM

ARCO DI CONSTANTINO
Built in AD 315 by the Senate and people of Rome, this grand arch celebrates Constantine's 312 victory over his rival Maxentius at the Milvian Bridge. An early recycling project, it took many of its marble bas reliefs from older monuments.

 D3 ✪35   PIAZZA DEL COLOSSEO

ARCO DI GIANO
This rare extant four-sided marble arch is dedicated to Janus, the major Roman god of ports, exits, entrances, and new beginnings (note "January" for the first month). This often-overlooked sight is built on the legendary spot where shepherd Faustolo discovered twins Romulus and Remus.

 D1 ✪32   PIAZZA DELLA BOCCA DELLA VERITÀ

BOCCA DELLA VERITÀ
Included in a famous scene in *Roman Holiday*, Bocca della Verità (Mouth of Truth) is said to bite the hand of liars. In

truth, it is an ancient marble drain cover with the mask of a river deity.

 D1 ✪31   PIAZZA DELLA BOCCA DELLA VERITÀ
06-67-81-419

DOMUS AUREA
When Nero's Golden House – built after the great fire of AD 64 – was rediscovered in the Renaissance, artists like Raphael flocked to see it, and a craze for grotesques (a word derived from the grotto where they were discovered) hit the world of interior design. A portion has been shut down since 2004 after a ceiling collapsed, but it's still worth a visit.

 D4 ✪38   VIALE DELLA DOMUS AUREA 1
06-39-96-77-00

FORUM BOARIUM
Forum Boarium, ancient Rome's meat market, contains the oldest marble temple standing in Rome: The round Temple of Hercules Vincitore (once attributed to Vesta) dates from the 2nd century BC.

 D1 ✪30   PIAZZA DELLA BOCCA DELLA VERITÀ

PALAZZO DEL QUIRINALE
Since 1947, this former papal residence has served as the residence of Italy's president. The square offers a splendid panorama and colossal statues of Castor and Pollux. The palace is open to the public on Sunday mornings if there are no diplomatic events.

 A2 ✪5   PIAZZA DEL QUIRINALE
06-46-991

SAN GIOVANNI IN LATERANO
Emperor Constantine wouldn't recognize this church he built in AD 313. Fire and religious fervor meant continual expansion and an opportunity for Borromini and Domenico Fontana to display their talents. The baptistery and cloisters are especially worth visiting for the mosaics.

MAP 5 E6 ✪45   PIAZZA DI SAN GIOVANNI IN LATERANO 4
06-77-26-641

SANTA MARIA IN COSMEDIN
Originally built in the 3rd century over a monument to Hercules, this Greek church shares its portico with the Bocca della Verità, but is also known for its Kosmidion decoration and elegant 12th-century bell tower.

 D1 ✪33   PIAZZA DELLA BOCCA DELLA VERITÀ
06-67-81-419

SANTI COSMA E DAMIANO
Admire art from different eras at this church: The mosaics date from the 6th and 7th centuries, while the Francesco Allegrini frescoes were added about 1,000 years later.

MAP 5 C2 ✪23   VIA DEI FORI IMPERIALI 1
'06-69-20-441

SCALA SANTA

Often mistakenly attributed to Pilate's palace in Jerusalem, these holy steps originally came from a local ceremonial palace. Today pilgrims ascend while kneeling; the steps lead to a chapel holding sacred relics that can be viewed behind a grate.

 E6✪44 PIAZZA DI SAN GIOVANNI IN LATERANO 14
06-77-26-641

 TRASTEVERE

COMPLESSO DELL' DEI CAVALIERI DI MALTA

This lovely walled complex offers a delightful optical illusion: Peep through the keyhole at no. 3 to see St. Peter's framed in miniature by the keyhole.

 E5✪29 PIAZZA DEI CAVALIERI DI MALTA

SANTA CECILIA

The tranquil beauty of the courtyard belies the goingson inside, where the artworks depict the death and martyrdom of Santa Cecilia, the patron saint of music. Roman officials first tried to steam Cecilia to death in her thermal baths; then they botched her beheading so it took her three days to die.

 C5✪24 PIAZZA SANTA CECILIA

SANTA MARIA IN TRASTEVERE

This church – considered to be the first in Rome dedicated to the Virgin Mary – is most notable for its mosaics. Its 12th-century facade features brilliant mosaics of Mary breastfeeding the baby Jesus, while inside, the mosaic tells the story of the Virgin. Fragments of rare 1st-century mosaics from Palestrina are on display, along with an equally rare 6th-century wooden painting of the Madonna.

 B2✪16 PIAZZA SANTA MARIA IN TRASTEVERE 06-58-97-352 OR 06-58-14-802

VATICANO

BASILICA DI SAN PIETRO

Basilica di San Pietro (St. Peter's Basilica) is the center of the Catholic Church and the world's largest Catholic church. It attracts devout pilgrims, as well as secular visitors who come to admire its monumental architecture, especially the magnificent dome and plaza.

In about AD 320, Emperor Constantine commissioned a basilica to be built over the tomb of the first pope, St.

SANTA MARIA IN TRASTEVERE   BASILICA DI SAN PIETRO

Peter, who was martyred in Nero's Circus. In the mid-15th century, a new church, mandated to be the seat of Roman Catholic power, was commissioned to replace the aging original structure. Bramante, Raphael, and Michelangelo all contributed their talents to the church's design and decoration. St. Peter's was finally consecrated in 1626, its 1,300th anniversary.

Today the basilica, though not technically part of the city, is Rome's most heavily trafficked tourist sight. After a long wait in line that slows to go through metal detectors, prepare to be scrutinized at the door for proper attire. Michelangelo's bullet-proof glass-encased *Pietà*, Arnolfo da Cambio's *St. Peter* (whose foot is shiny from touches and kisses), and Bernini's *Baldecchino* are all inside, under enormous mosaics that at first appear to be paintings. You can tour the church's immense brick dome by walking up a treacherous staircase or by taking the elevator part of the way. The observation deck outside allows you to survey the Eternal City, while the gallery provides an aerial view of the basilica's interior.

SIDE WALKS

If you have time and energy after a trip to the Vatican, you may want to explore the offerings nearby.

Savelli Arte e Tradizione (p. 60), right outside St. Peter's Square, is a good place to stop for quality religious souvenirs.

You may not be in the mood for more museums, but **Museo Storico Nazionale dell'Arte Sanitaria (p. 68)** holds fascinating displays of medical artifacts.

Right across the Tiber, numerous dining and entertainment options lie in the area verging on Piazza Navona, such as **Pierluigi (p. 38),** a hot spot with Italian fare.

Check to see if **Oratorio del Gonfalone (p. 74)** has any concerts – it's a romantic spot to wind down the day.

C2✪22   PIAZZA DI SAN PIETRO 06-69-88-37-12 OR 06-69-88-44-66
HOURS: DAILY 7 AM–7 PM

CASTEL SANT'ANGELO

Mausoleum, fortress, prison, and papal residence, the round Castel Sant'Angelo once protected popes during times of war and invasion; today it guards a rich past that dates back to the 2nd century.

The building's history began in AD 123, when Emperor Hadrian commissioned it as a tomb for himself and future emperors. Then, for more than 1,000 years it served as a fortress for the city's papal leaders – it has a secret corridor built above the wall to connect the castle to the Vatican for quick getaways. (As a fortress, it was a strategic point of defense, and Pope Urban V noted that he who controlled the keys to the castle controlled Rome.) The structure received its current name in AD 590, when Pope Gregory the Great reported seeing an angel on the roof of the castle. In the vision, the angel was sheathing his sword, an act that Gregory interpreted as a divine sign that the plague raging in Rome was over. A sculpture of that vision sits atop the building.

Periodically during its history, the castle was also used as a prison and, no doubt, a torture chamber. Giordano Bruno, the heretic burned at the stake in 1600, was incarcerated here. Beatrice Cenci, who became the protagonist of Percy Bysshe Shelley's verse drama *The Cenci*, was executed nearby.

As visitors enter Castel Sant'Angelo, they see the original door to Hadrian's tomb. Once inside, a ramp leads to the cell where the 2nd-century emperor's ashes were kept. The papal apartments are open to the public and are decorated with 15th- and 16th-century frescoes that hint at the luxury in which many of the popes lived. The terraces offer sweeping views of the city below. The café offers a good view of the *passetto* and is ideal for viewing St. Peter's dome at sunset.

 MAP 7 C5●28   LUNGOTEVERE CASTELLO 50 • 06-39-96-76-00 OR 06-68-19-111
HOURS: TUES.-SUN. 9 AM-8 PM

MUSEI VATICANI/CAPPELLA SISTINA

The world's most famous ceiling is the crown jewel in a chapel that already had a beautiful cycle of frescoes that dated to 1481-1483, when great artists of the day like Botticelli, Pinturicchio, and Perugino were called in to paint.

The Cappella Sistina's (Sistine Chapel) second phase of frescoes painted by Michelangelo are among the

Western world's most impressive art – and by a man who considered himself to be a sculptor, not a painter. Michelangelo began work in 1508 and completed it in 1512, working alone upon scaffolding. Images cover the entire ceiling of the chapel and one wall, and they tell the story of humankind before the birth of Christ through nine primary panels. The ceiling frescoes portray, in order from the altar, the Separation of Light from Darkness, the Creation of the Heavenly Bodies, the Separation of Land and Sea, the Creation of Adam, the Creation of Eve, the Fall of Man and the Expulsion from Paradise, the Flood, the Sacrifice of Noah, and the Drunkenness of Noah. Michelangelo returned 24 years later to paint the altar wall with the final scene, The Last Judgment. During the early 1990s, expert restorers cleaned the chapel's frescoes, revealing much more vibrant color than it had shown for hundreds of years.

In order to get to the chapel, a traipse through the Musei Vaticani (Vatican Museums) is required. It's not a chore, though, as the museums within this vast compound are fascinating and range from Egyptian, Etruscan, Greek, and Roman art to 16th-century maps. For sheer size of collection, as well as the quality of the works, no museum in town can compete with the Vatican. Its strength can also be its weakness, though: long lines to get inside the building, no "shortcuts" to the Sistine Chapel, and seeing the minimum may even take half a day as you shuffle slowly through courtyards, up stairways, and down corridors. Note that the entrance is located on Viale Vaticano – trying to access the museums from some other point will result in a long walk to the correct entrance.

 B2 16 VIALE VATICANO 100 • 06-69-88-38-60 OR 06-69-88-43-41; HOURS: MON.-FRI. 8:45 AM-3:20 PM; SAT. AND LAST SUN. OF THE MONTH 8:45 AM-12:20 PM (NOV.-FEB.)

PONTE SANT'ANGELO
Lined with angels sculpted by followers of Bernini, the Sant'Angelo is one of the city's most beautiful bridges.

MAP 7 **C5 29** LUNGOTEVERE CASTELLO

TERME DI CARACALLA

The ritual of bathing in ancient Rome was not unlike the spa culture in the United States today – both involve relaxation through cleansing. However, in ancient times, fees for access to the baths were nominal (everyone but slaves could afford them), and soap had not yet been invented. When they were completed in AD 212, the Baths (Terme) of Caracalla were the largest built in Rome, and they remained open until 537 when Goths cut the aqueduct leading to the baths.

In AD 206, Emperor Septimius Severus began building the baths and his son, Caracalla, completed them. The facilities could accommodate 1,600 bathers simultaneously, as bathing was a social activity. The caldarium was a room that was both hot and humid. Since there was no soap, scrapers were used for the job of removing dirt. The tepidarium was, as the name suggests, a room for cooling down slowly, whereas the frigidarium was more like a cold plunge-pool. As for tubs, two enormous granite tubs from Caracalla can be seen today in Piazza Farnese.

The complex also included large gyms where visitors could exercise and get massaged, waxed, and pampered to a buff state. There were common areas and gardens for strolling, as well as art galleries, concert halls, and Greek and Latin libraries.

The current site only hints at what was here before. Still standing are parts of stone walls that once designated the frigidarium, tepidarium, and other exercise and meeting spaces. Mosaics that tiled pool floors can also be seen in the gymnasia. Sometimes an English-speaking guide can be booked by phoning ahead. Don't miss a chance to see a performance here in summer, now on again after having been banned for years.

OVERVIEW MAP **E4** VIALE DELLE TERME DI CARACALLA 52 • 06-39-96-7700 HOURS: DAILY 9 AM-6 PM (APR.-SEP.); MON. 9 AM-1 PM; TUES.-SUN. 9 AM-3:30 PM (SEP.-MAR.)

LA PIRAMIDE DI CAIO CESTIO

This may not rival the Pyramid of Cheops, but the Pyramid of Caio Cesto nevertheless is a surprise on the horizon to travelers in the south end of the city. It was constructed as a funerary monument to Caio Cestio Epulone soon after his death in 12 BC.

OVERVIEW MAP **F3** PIAZZALE OSTIENSE

R RESTAURANTS

Hottest restaurant of the moment: **CRUDO**, p. 24

Most fashionable dolce vita spot: **'GUSTO**, p. 30

Best wine selection: **ENOTECA FERRARA**, p. 36

Best place to eat as the Romans eat:
CHECCHINO DAL 1887, p. 38

Best gelato: **IL GELATO DI SAN CRISPINO**, p. 29

Best pizzeria: **DA BAFFETTO**, p. 27

Most romantic: **EL TOULÀ**, p. 29

Best splurge: **LA PERGOLA**, p. 38

Best view with a meal: **LA TERRAZZA DELL'EDEN**, p. 32

Best alfresco dining:
LA VERANDA DEL'HOTEL COLUMBUS, p. 38

MAP 1 GHETTO/CAMPO DEI FIORI

ACQUA NEGRA *HOT SPOT • MEDITERRANEAN* $$
Cosmopolitan describes both the restaurant and its patrons.
Whether enjoying creative Italian fare or sampling exotic libations,
the crowd is always relaxed and hip. The water theme is evident in
both the wine cellar-like selection of bottled water and the water-
fall near the restrooms.

MAP 1 B3 **R** 12   LARGO DEL TEATRO VALLE 9
06-97-60-60-26

AL BRIC *ROMANTIC • ITALIAN* $$
On the whimsical menu at this intimate restaurant, you might find
hot-and-sour Thai soup next to homemade tagliatelle with *fiore
di zucca* (zucchini blossoms). Owner Roberto Marchetti promises
that the often organic ingredients are the freshest available, and
his extensive wine list is a bargain.

MAP 1 B1 **R** 8   VIA DEL PELLEGRINO 51
06-68-79-533

CAFFÈ FARNESE *AFTER HOURS • ITALIAN* $
In an elegant piazza steps away from the madness of Campo dei
Fiori, Caffè Farnese is a great place to while away the hours over
coffee by day and cocktails by night. The food, mainly sandwiches
and salads, is secondary to the experience.

MAP 1 C1 **R** 17   VIA DEI BAULLARI 106
06-68-80-21-25

CRUDO *HOT SPOT • INTERNATIONAL* $$
The name means "raw" in Italian, and that's what you'll get here –
seafood and meat carpaccio, sushi, sashimi, and fresh vegetables
with Mediterranean flair. But the real draw is the raw, artist-studio
feel, with obscure art and video installations creating a funky, con-
vivial atmosphere.

MAP 1 D3 **R** 32   VIA DEGLI SPECCHI 6
06-68-38-989

DA GIGGETTO *HOT SPOT • ITALIAN* $$
This torchbearer for Jewish-Italian cooking serves loyal regu-
lars who dine on fried zucchini flowers in season, and *baccalà*
(salt cod) and artichokes (prepared *alla giudea* – flattened and
pan-fried) year-round. If you come in a second time, servers will
remember and ask your name.

MAP 1 E5 **R** 37   VIA DEL PORTICO D'OTTAVIA 21A
06-68-61-105

FILETTI DI BACCALÀ *QUICK BITES • ITALIAN* $
This Roman institution, somewhat of a dive, specializes in one
thing and one thing only: greaselessly fried salt cod fillets, served
with *puntarelle,* a local chicory, in winter. There are other items on
the menu, but few people seem to notice.

MAP 1 C2 **R** 24   LARGO DEI LIBRARI 88
06-68-64-018

TRADITIONAL ROMAN FOOD

Rome's cuisine is bold, savory, and full of fresh, local ingredients. Pecorino Romano, a hard, sheep's milk cheese, is *materia prima* in many traditional pasta dishes: It's grated into a hearty mix of eggs and *pancetta* (bacon) in *spaghetti alla carbonara*; shaved over *bucatini all'amatriciana*'s spicy, smoky sauce of tomatoes, onions, and pancetta; or simply and deliciously paired with black pepper in *cacio e pepe*. Artichokes, or *carcioffi*, are prepared *alla Romana* with mint, garlic, and white wine, or *alla giudia* (flattened and crisply fried). Colorful zucchini flowers, stuffed with mozzarella and anchovies, make a decadent, deep-fried starter. Meat dishes feature lamb, tripe, or veal – as in *saltimbocca* (jump in the mouth), which is topped with Parma ham and sage. As for the Roman staple pizza, the local version is thin crusted and best with simple toppings like tomatoes, basil, and buffalo mozzarella. If your mouth is watering by now, try these dishes at their best at **Matricianella (p. 30), Panattoni (p. 36),** and **Checchino dal 1887 (p. 38).**

IL FORNO DI CAMPO DEI FIORI *QUICK BITES • PIZZA* $
Here locals line up for pizza by the slice. Among the city's best for *al taglio* squares, this small, crowded favorite serves them up as big or as small as you want, topped in fresh ingredients and often hot from the oven. The staff is always harried but couldn't be friendlier.

 C1 🄡19   PIAZZA CAMPO DEI FIORI 22
06-68-80-66-62

PIPERNO *FAMOUS • ROMAN* $$
Sunday brunch is the only early meal served, but it's a must on any vacation itinerary for its hearty offerings. Otherwise, traditional Roman-Jewish dishes – fried zucchini flowers, *baccalà*, and artichokes – come in bountiful and shareable portions. Outdoor seating in the small piazza is delightful.

 E4 🄡35   VIA MONTE DEI CENCI 9
06-68-80-66-29

VECCHIA LOCANDA *ROMANTIC • ITALIAN/ROMAN* $$
This restaurant has been going strong since 1930, thanks to its faithfulness to Roman culinary tradition – you won't find a better bowl of *bucatini all'amatriciana*. The peaceful, candlelit room is a refuge in the heart of one of the city's busiest areas.

 B4 🄡14   VICOLO SINIBALDI 2
06-68-80-28-31

CAFFÈ SANT'EUSTACHIO

MYOSOTIS

VINERIA   *AFTER HOURS • WINE BAR* $

This quintessential Roman wine bar in Campo dei Fiori is a prime people-watching spot. The bartenders give generous pours of wine and cocktails, and securing a table outside makes you feel like all is right with the world, if only for an hour.

 C1 **R20**   PIAZZA CAMPO DEI FIORI 15
06-68-80-32-68

ZÌ FENIZIA   *QUICK BITES • PIZZA* $

Rome's only kosher pizzeria, the house specialty here is *aciughe e indivia* (anchovies and endive). If that doesn't tempt you, there are 39 other flavors to choose from by the slice. Take it to go, or wedge in to the crowded standing-room-only area.

 D4 **R33**   VIA SANTA MARIA DEL PIANTO 64
06-68-96-976

 PIAZZA NAVONA/PANTHEON

CAFFÈ SANT'EUSTACHIO   *CAFÉ* $

This café is among the most famous in Rome. The superb house-roasted beans are for sale, along with coffee-based confections. Baristas will add sugar to your espresso unless you say otherwise. Finding a spot at the crowded serving bar or a table can be a gladiator's challenge.

 C3 **R42**   PIAZZA SANT'EUSTACHIO 82
06-68-80-20-48

IL CONVIVIO   *BUSINESS • ITALIAN* $$

The brothers who own Convivio offer quality food with top-rate service. The elaborate and creative dishes include a simply perfect prawn and green bean salad, porcini mushroom risotto, and scalloped quail. Satisfy your sweet tooth with an original tiramisu with strawberries and bananas.

 A2 **R5**   VICOLO DEI SOLDATI 31
06-68-69-432

CUL DE SAC   *AFTER HOURS • WINE BAR* $

Cul de Sac's encyclopedic wine list may make your head spin, even

before one of their wines has a chance to. The friendly staff can help
you navigate the regional and international selections, offered by
the bottle and the glass. Coveted outdoor tables are worth the wait.

 MAP 2 C2 ℝ40 PIAZZA DI PASQUINO 73
06-68-80-10-94

DA BAFFETTO *QUICK BITES • PIZZA* $
The line of Romans hovering at the door is the give-away that this
is one of the top pizzerias in town. The service can be brusque, but
the traditional, thin-crust pizza with standard toppings like mozzarella and tomatoes with basil somehow makes you forget all that.

 MAP 2 C1 ℝ37 VIA DEL GOVERNO VECCHIO 114
06-68-61-617

DA FRANCESCO *AFTER HOURS • PIZZA* $
This often-crowded Roman favorite is known for its typical thin-
crust pizzas, but you won't go wrong sampling the antipasto bar,
which features Italian delights like grilled vegetables, stuffed
tomatoes, and frittatas, or filling up on one of the pastas. Warm
weather brings tables out onto the popular piazza.

MAP 2 B1 ℝ16 PIAZZA DEL FICO 29
06-68-64-009

GIOLITTI *QUICK BITES • GELATO* $
Frequently appearing on locals' short list for best gelaterie, Giolitti
offers its cold desserts in a selective number of mouthwatering
seasonal flavors. The best are *nocciòla* (hazelnut) and *fragola*
(strawberry).

 MAP 2 A5 ℝ13 VIA DEGLI UFFICI DEL VICARIO 40
06-69-91-243

HOSTARIA DELL'ORSO *ROMANTIC • ITALIAN* $$$
An elegant, historic palazzo is the setting for this special-occa-
sion restaurant. After savoring one of the five tasting menus,
which include fish, rabbit, and delicate antipasti, sip after-dinner
drinks in the piano bar. When the kitchen closes, the chic night-
club upstairs opens.

 MAP 2 A2 ℝ4 VIA DEI SOLDATI 25C
06-68-30-11-92

MACCHERONI *HOT SPOT • ITALIAN/ROMAN* $$
Maccheroni is regularly packed with groups of young, fashionable
locals who fill up on the good Roman food (staple pasta dishes
include *amatriciana* and *cacio e pepe*) before heading out for a
night on the town.

 MAP 2 A4 ℝ11 PIAZZA DELLE COPPELLE 44
06-68-30-78-95

MYOSOTIS *HOT SPOT • ITALIAN* $$
One of Rome's first restaurants to explore *cucina nuova*, Myosotis
now has a strong hold on locals and tourists alike with its near-
Pantheon address and perennially inventive food. Handmade
pasta and fish are always good choices, and the desserts are
refreshingly light, almost healthy.

 MAP 2 A4 ℝ10 VICOLO DELLA VACCARELLA 3
06-68-65-554

LA ROSETTA TAZZA D'ORO GINA

RICCIOLI *AFTER HOURS • INTERNATIONAL* $$

If Massimo Riccioli's La Rosetta is too steep for your budget, head around the corner to his more casual but terminally chic bar/restaurant. Japan meets Italy in this mod space, serving sushi, oysters, and seafood to Fendi-wearing hipsters and body-conscious it-girls until 2 AM.

  A4 **R12** PIAZZA DELLE COPPELLE 10A
06-68-21-03-13

LA ROSETTA *ROMANTIC • SEAFOOD* $$$

This elegant, high-class restaurant is considered one of the best for fish in the entire city. Tasting menus are the best way to experience the kitchen's range, which spans simple grilled catch to light pastas with shellfish. All are delicious and unimaginably fresh.

 B4 **R30** VIA DELLA ROSETTA 8
06-68-61-002

SALOTTO 42 *CAFÉ* $

Salotto is Italian for "living room," appropriate for the library-chic decor and novella-sized menu of teas, coffee drinks, and cocktails. And it's a room with a view: Gaze across to the 2nd-century Temple of Hadrian from your comfy sofa cushion.

 B6 **R35** PIAZZA DI PIETRA 42
06-67-85-804

SANTA LUCIA *HOT SPOT • ITALIAN* $$

Almost all the seats here are outdoors under mature trees decorated with lights. The food is equally creative, light, and mostly healthy, with small course options for those who don't want a huge meal. Fish dishes from the Amalfi Coast is a specialty.

 A2 **R8** LARGO FEBO 12
06-68-80-24-27

TAZZA D'ORO *CAFÉ* $

Competing with Caffè Sant'Eustachio for the Best-in-Rome title, Tazza d'Oro packs in serious coffee drinkers – many of them politicos from the nearby senate building – who down espresso standing up at the bar. The *coffee granita* (shaved ice) with homemade whipped cream is a must.

 B5 **R33** VIA D'ORFANI 84
06-67-89-792

MAP 3 | TRIDENTE

BABINGTON'S TEA ROOMS *BREAKFAST AND BRUNCH • TEA* $$
An elegant place to get a spot o' tea, Babington's also serves pancakes and bacon until 11 AM. Tea service – formal and on the expensive side – is steeped in history at this spot where British expats like Keats and Shelley once lounged.

MAP 3 D5 ⓡ42 PIAZZA DI SPAGNA 23
06-67-86-027

IL BRILLO PARLANTE *AFTER HOURS • WINE BAR* $
The best place for a snack or light meal near Piazza del Popolo, this wine bar and café pours 20 wines by the glass and serves salads, pastas, and grilled meats in inviting wood-paneled rooms.

MAP 3 B3 ⓡ9 VIA DELLA FONTANELLA 12
06-32-43-334

DA MARIO *BUSINESS • ITALIAN* $$
Here, the owner dines among tourists and natives alike, all feasting on the hearty Roman and Tuscan fare. Walls are cluttered with photos of famous patrons – mostly Italians – a testament to the authenticity of the savory dishes and to one of the best tiramisus in town.

MAP 3 D5 ⓡ48 VIA DELLA VITE 55
06-67-83-818

EL TOULÀ *ROMANTIC • ITALIAN* $$$
El Toulà is an elegant bastion of hospitality, where service is as important as food. The restaurant is a Roman institution, as are its signature dishes: *fegato alla veneziana* (sweet-and-sour liver) and *baccalà mantecato* (salt cod whipped with milk). Elegant dress recommended.

MAP 3 E2 ⓡ52 VIA DELLA LUPA 29B
06-68-73-750

IL GELATO DI SAN CRISPINO *QUICK BITES • GELATO* $
A favorite among favorites, San Crispino is so serious about gelato that you aren't allowed to eat it in a cone, as the flavor might be compromised. Sample a cup of renowned creations like balsamic vinegar, 32-year-old whiskey, Marsala wine, or honey cream.

MAP 3 F5 ⓡ71 VIA DELLA PANETTERIA 42
06-67-93-924

GINA *HOT SPOT • ITALIAN* $$
Posh picnics for two are prepared at this all-white eatery, complete with basket, tablecloth, glasses, *panini,* fruit salad, dessert, and coffee – perfect for an alfresco lunch in the nearby Borghese Gardens. Prefer to eat inside? Gina offers breakfast, lunch, and dinner (pasta, sandwiches, and salads are the standard fare) 8 AM–midnight.

MAP 3 C5 ⓡ28 VIA SAN SEBASTIANELLO 7A
06-67-80-251

'GUSTO *HOT SPOT • ITALIAN* $$

'Gusto is a foodie's heaven: Two floors of dining options – from informal pizzas and pastas downstairs to gourmet fare upstairs – an expertly stocked wine bar, and a kitchen store with cookbooks and every conceivable culinary gadget are all found inside this warehouse-like compound in the heart of the city.

MAP 3 C2 ℝ18 PIAZZA AUGUSTO IMPERATORE 7/9
06-32-266-273

HAMASEI *BUSINESS • JAPANESE* $$

Hands-down the best Japanese restaurant in Rome, Hamasei is an oasis of calm in the middle of the buzzing Tridente. Waiters speak Japanese, Italian, and English, and the menu, as well as the service, is traditional Japanese.

MAP 3 E5 ℝ60 VIA DELLA MERCEDE 35-36
06-67-92-134

HOTEL DE RUSSIE *BREAKFAST AND BRUNCH* $$

The food at the garden courtyard inside this luxurious hotel might make you wonder if you're really in Rome: Traditional English and American breakfasts are available, as are bran muffins and smoothies. Italian *cornetti* (croissants) are an option for when-in-Rome adherents.

MAP 3 A3 ℝ5 VIA DEL BABUINO 9
06-32-88-81

MATRICIANELLA *BUSINESS • ITALIAN/ROMAN* $$

It's known for traditional Roman dishes such as *pasta amatriciana* and roasted lamb, as well as for flavorful desserts like oranges in cinnamon and wine or pears in Barolo. This politicians' and businessmen's haunt may require serious negotiation to get a table without a reservation.

MAP 3 E3 ℝ54 VIA DEL LEONE 2/4
06-68-32-100

NON SOLO BEVI *QUICK BITES • WINE BAR* $

Located in an elegant piazza off chaotic Via del Corso, this is an inexpensive oasis in Rome's priciest shopping district. Outdoor-only seating makes it a prime spot for people-watching, sipping wine or coffee, or eating tasty sandwiches before heading to nearby Piazza di Spagna.

MAP 3 E3 ℝ55 PIAZZA SAN LORENZO IN LUCINA 15
06-68-71-683

OBIKÀ *HOT SPOT • ITALIAN* $

Rome's – and perhaps the world's – first "mozzarella bar" dishes up tastings of buffalo mozzarella from the country's best producers. Served with flavorful chutneys, in light salads or between tempting sandwiches, the fresh selections make this a favorite lunch spot for nearby politicians and savvy vegetarians.

MAP 3 E2 ℝ53 VIA DEI PREFETTI 26A
06-68-32-630

RECAFÉ *HOT SPOT • PIZZA* $$

The minimalist atmosphere attracts a stylish Roman crowd, as do the more than two dozen varieties of thick-crust, Neapolitan-

APERITIVO

Italian happy hour is a good way to enjoy the ambience at some of Rome's most stylish spots for cheap. Starting at about 7:30 PM, *aperitivo* is a bubbling social hour for sipping wine or *prosecco* and grazing on delectable little dishes before dinner at 9 PM. Lounges and restaurants lay out a mini-buffet ranging from crudités, potato chips, and nuts to light pasta dishes, tiny kebabs, and small sandwiches. The food is free and mostly unlimited with your drink order, usually ranging €5-10 ($6-12). At sleek **Riccioli (p. 28),** you can make a meal of their sushi, sashimi, and couscous dishes — even if you only order a cranberry juice of €4 ($5). **Crudo (p. 24)** is the pre-dinner place for the in-crowd, where they nosh on seafood, pastas, and assorted savories. **Acqua Negra (p. 24)** is another hip address to snack on salami, pastas, and lamb skewers, while sipping an exotic lychee martini.

style pizza (most under €10/$12 and on Wednesdays the price drops to €6/$7.20). Salads, pastas, and meat dishes are also served in this multilevel eatery.

 D3 **R**30 PIAZZA AUGUSTO IMPERATORE 36
06-68-13-47-30

RISTORANTE DAL BOLOGNESE *HOT SPOT • ITALIAN $$*
Despite its Piazza del Popolo location, this restaurant caters to politicos more than shoppers. Headliners are the tagliatelle with truffles, herbed tuna tartar, and *pappardelle* with duck ragout — all staple dishes from Bologna. Finish off in the cigar salon where you can sample the selection of spirits.

MAP**3** A2 **R**2 PIAZZA DEL POPOLO 1-2
06-36-11-426

ROMAN GARDEN LOUNGE *ROMANTIC • MEDITERRANEAN $$$*
Homemade ravioli, fresh fish, and seasonal vegetables prepared in various Mediterranean styles headline at Hotel d'Inghilterra's restaurant. Most diners come laden with shopping bags and use the elegant yet noisy space to refresh and refuel.

MAP**3** D4 **R**39 HOTEL D'INGHILTERRA, VIA BOCCA DI LEONE 14
06-69-98-11

THÈ VERDE *CAFÉ $*
This Zen, teatime retreat near Piazza di Spagna offers tea varieties from around the world, which you can sip in the enclosed patio. Thè Verde serves light lunches and sweets, and sells Eastern-inspired home accessories and fashion as well as brew-it-yourself tea.

MAP**3** C4 **R**25 VIA BOCCA DI LEONE 46
06-69-92-37-05

MAP 4 | **VIA VENETO/TERMINI**

AFRICA   *QUICK BITES • ETHIOPIAN* $

Specialties at this refuge for the pasta- and pizza-weary include *zighini* (spicy beef) and *sambussa* (minced meat logs), eaten by hand using the spongy, sour *injera* bread. It's also open for traditional yogurt-based breakfasts, a welcome change from Rome's usual sweet pastries.

 D4 **Ⓡ26**   VIA GAETA 26
06-49-41-077

GRAN CAFFÈ DONEY   *CAFÉ* $$

Part of the Westin Excelsior Hotel, the red, black, and gold Doney has elegant banquettes inside and café tables outside, right on Via Veneto. By day, sip a cappuccino at a streetside table, and by night, join the see-and-be-seen crowd of young Roman socialites for the cocktail hour.

 C2 **Ⓡ8**   WESTIN EXCELSIOR HOTEL, VIA VENETO 145
06-47-08-28-25

MONTE CARUSO   *ROMANTIC • ITALIAN* $$

Southern Italian food takes center stage in this stucco-arched, terra cotta–floored space. The stuffed pasta dishes – like the rigatoni and cannelloni – are as good as a trip to Basilicata or Calabria, and the service could not be more gracious.

 F4 **Ⓡ38**   VIA FARINI 12
06-48-35-49

PAPÀ BACCUS   *HOT SPOT • ITALIAN* $$$

A simultaneously upmarket and homey Tuscan restaurant just off Via Veneto, Papà Baccus grills its famous *bistecche fiorentine* (T-bone steak) and serves it simply with olive oil and salt. Wonderful side dishes might include hearty white beans in olive oil and herbs or roasted potatoes.

 B2 **Ⓡ3**   VIA TOSCANA 36
06-42-74-28-08

LE SANS SOUCI   *HOT SPOT • FRENCH/ITALIAN* $$$

Le Sans Souci hosts see-and-be-seen diners in elegant banquettes and serves a fusion of French and Italian classics. Its Michelin star was earned with dishes like lobster with black truffles and over-the-top desserts such as the decadent chocolate soufflé.

 C2 **Ⓡ7**   VIA SICILIA 20
06-48-21-814

LA TERRAZZA DELL'EDEN   *ROMANTIC • INTERNATIONAL* $$$

With commanding views of Rome and an interior of refined candlelit elegance, La Terrazza is a sight in itself. Dishes like cauliflower flan with oyster tempura; gnocchi with eggplant, ricotta, and balsamic vinegar; and roasted lamb characterize the simply designed choices. The rosemary gelato makes a refreshing dessert.

MAP4 C1 **Ⓡ5**   VIA LUDOVISI 49
06-47-81-21

MONTE CARUSO

LA TERRAZZA DELL'EDEN

TRIMANI WINE BAR   *AFTER HOURS • WINE BAR $*
Run by the folks who own the food shop of the same name,
Trimani serves interesting dishes like mushroom and chestnut
soup or *baccalà* meatballs. But the prime feature is the list of at
least 15 wines by the glass, and for those who want more, the shop
conducts tastings and classes. Closed in August.

 C4 VIA CERNAIA 37B
06-44-69-630

  COLOSSEO

AGATA & ROMEO   *HOT SPOT • ITALIAN/ROMAN $$$*
In a neighborhood lacking fine dining choices, Agata & Romeo is a
shining beacon of edible excellence, serving up a seasonally rotat-
ing menu of traditional Roman food and creative alternatives. On
the menu, tuna burgers with soy sauce sit alongside ravioli with
potatoes, rosemary, and the fatty Italian delicacy, *lardo*.

 B5 20 VIA CARLO ALBERTO 45
06-44-66-115

L'ANTICA BIRRERIA PERONI   *QUICK BITES • ITALIAN $*
At this *birreria* of Italy's most-exported beer, you can try all the
brews not available worldwide, like the Gran Riserva, a voluptuous
beer that goes perfectly with the hearty food served here, like
roasted pork, hot dogs, and beef stew. The space is a true beer
hall, down to the communal seating.

MAP 5 A1 R4 VIA SAN MARCELLO 19
06-67-95-310

CAVOUR 313   *AFTER HOURS • WINE BAR $*
One of Rome's first wine bars, Cavour is a homey spot for a pre-
dinner date or a light snack. Here you can always find the perfect
cheese or salad to accompany your choice of the 25 wines avail-
able by the glass.

 C3 R26 VIA CAVOUR 313
06-67-85-496

F.I.S.H.   *HOT SPOT • INTERNATIONAL* $$$

The Fine International Seafood House is one of the reasons why
the funky Monti neighborhood – in the shadow of the Colosseum –
is a favorite of the young and hip. It lives up to its name, with
a slick oyster and sushi bar and a Mediterranean, Asian, and
Oceanic menu.

 VIA DEI SERPENTI 16
06-47-82-49-62

MAHARAJAH   *HOT SPOT • INDIAN* $$

In a city where the quality of ethnic food is mediocre at best,
Maharajah stands out. Its lavishly carved decor and ornate table
settings don't distract from the excellent tandoori delights, fluffy
naan, spicy-sweet chutneys, and crispy *pakora*.

 VIA DEI SERPENTI 124
06-47-47-144

PANELLA   *QUICK BITES • BAKERY* $

Panella's bakers are passionate about bread, studying ancient
techniques and recipes to turn out more than 80 simple and gourmet varieties. Their ovens also produce savory tarts and delicate
pastries, displayed among regional snacks not available else-
where. It's also great for on-the-go lunches.

 VIA MERULANA 54-55
06-48-72-344

SAN TEODORO   *BUSINESS • ITALIAN* $$

One of the few quality restaurants near the Colosseum, San
Teodoro is famous for its *carciofi alla giudea* (fried baby artichokes). Other nicely prepared dishes include homemade ravioli
and a fresh fish of the day. Try to sit on the fabulous, bustling
patio.

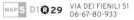 VIA DEI FIENILI 51
06-67-80-933

TRATTORIA MONTI   *ROMANTIC • ITALIAN* $$

The Camerucci family runs this friendly place, located a short walk
from the Colosseum. Verdicchio, the most famous white wine from
the owners' home region of the Marches, is served along with all
manner of soups, stews, and fish dishes.

 VIA SAN VITO 13A
06-44-66-573

ZEST   *BREAKFAST AND BRUNCH* $$

Atop the Radisson SAS hotel, Zest has a sweet and savory brunch
buffet – quiches, pastries, and light pastas – in the modern salon
or by the sleek pool. The skyscraping locale offers sweeping views
of Rome, as well as cocktails and dinner in the evening.

 VIA FILIPPO TURATI 171
06-44-48-41

MAP 6 | TRASTEVERE

ALBERTO CIARLA *HOT SPOT • SEAFOOD* $$$
Perpetually vying for the crown of top fish restaurant in the city, Alberto Ciarla is from a bygone era. Servers are formal and eminently versed in the day's catch and its subtle preparation, often as simple as sea bass with fresh herbs.

MAP 6 C2 R19 PIAZZA SAN COSIMATO 40
06-58-18-668

ASINOCOTTO *ROMANTIC • ITALIAN* $$
The only openly gay-owned restaurant in Rome welcomes gourmets of all persuasions with cutting-edge dishes like zucchini blossoms stuffed with green ricotta and homemade chocolate gelato with celery syrup. Wines offered by the glass are reflect Italy's regions and complement the light menu.

MAP 6 C5 R23 VIA DEI VASCELLARI 48
06-58-98-985

AUGUSTO *QUICK BITES • ITALIAN/ROMAN* $
Traditional Roman food, like pasta with lentils and shredded roasted pork, is dished out as if you were in an authentic Roman home. Locals line up outside and pack the tightly fitted tables inside this small, noisy spot, but everyone leaves well fed for less than $10.

MAP 6 B2 R13 PIAZZA DEI RENZI 15
06-58-03-798

IL CANTINIERE DI SANTA DOROTEA *AFTER HOURS • WINE BAR* $
Open until 2 AM (late by Roman standards), this welcoming cantina serves 35 wines by the glass in all price ranges. The menu always features at least one soup and a variety of *salumi* (cold cuts) and salads. Service is swift, but you are free to linger.

MAP 6 A2 R1 VIA DI SANTA DOROTEA 9
06-58-19-025

IL CIAK *HOT SPOT • ITALIAN* $$
This meat-lovers haven grills up thick Tuscan steaks, hearty wild boar, and other game. Start with *pappardelle* pasta in tomato and wild boar sauce, followed by a steak filet topped with shaved *parmigiano* and arugula. Good wine and homemade desserts come next. Reservations are essential.

MAP 6 A2 R8 VICOLO DEL CINQUE 21
06-58-94-774

DA CHECCO ER CARRETTIERE *FAMOUS • ITALIAN/ROMAN* $$
With braids of garlic hanging over the tables and checked tablecloths, this may look like many Italian restaurants in the States, but it's one of the best traditional restaurants in Rome. Don't miss the *bucatini all'amatriciana* (hollow spaghetti with a tomato, pancetta, and onion sauce).

MAP 6 A2 R3 VIA BENEDETTA 10
06-58-17-018

ENOTECA FERRARA   INSALATA RICCA

ENOTECA FERRARA *AFTER HOURS • WINE BAR* $$
The offerings at this casual restaurant/wine bar change weekly
and range from small snack-sized portions (herbed chèvre with
dates and pears) to full-on meals (sesame-crusted tuna fillets).
Servers are well versed in the encyclopedic wine list, which has
selections from every region in Italy, and make you feel right at
home.

 A2 **R**4 PIAZZA TRILUSSA 41
06-58-03-769

PANATTONI *QUICK BITES • PIZZA* $
Panattoni earned the nickname L'Obitorio (the morgue) for the
marble slabs upon which it makes some of the finest pizza in
Rome. The thin crust with simple toppings draws constant crowds,
as do fried *baccala* filets (salt cod) and *suppli* (fried rice balls with
a gooey mozzarella center).

 C4 **R**22 VIALE TRASTEVERE 53
06-58-00-919

SORA LELLA *ROMANTIC • ITALIAN/ROMAN* $$
The menu at this Isola Tiberina eatery may change daily, but the
homey atmosphere, with traditional Roman food to match, is a
dependable constant. The worn-in wood-paneled rooms look like
they could tell some fascinating stories, if their walls could talk.

 B5 **R**18 VIA PONTE QUATTRO CAPI 16
06-68-61-601

TRATTORIA DEGLI AMICI *AFTER HOURS • ITALIAN/ROMAN* $
Dedicated to hiring people with disabilities, Trattoria Degli Amici
serves simple Roman standards, such as chickpea soup, roasted
pork, and pasta with mussels, pesto, and zucchini, along with well-
selected wines and sweets made in-house – all at good prices.

 B2 **R**15 PIAZZA DI SANT'EGIDIO 6
06-58-06-033

VATICANO

IL BICCHIERE DI MASTAI *HOT SPOT • WINE BAR* $$

Chef-owner Fabio Baldassarre worked in Heinz Beck's La Pergola before opening this petite wine bar. The list is sophisticated and selective, with offerings by the glass. A refined variety of cheeses and cured meats are standards on the frequently rotating menu, which features items that range from fennel salad to smoked duck.

 D6 **R30** VIA DEI BANCHI NUOVI 52
06-68-19-22-28

CAFFÈ NOVECENTO *CAFÉ* $

Tarts, quiches, pastries, and salads accompany a long list of teas, coffee drinks, and juices at this lovely café. Located along one of the best shopping streets in Rome, it's a good place to charge up for a day of shopping or refuel during breaks.

 D6 **R32** VIA DEL GOVERNO VECCHIO 127
06-68-65-424

DAL TOSCANO *ROMANTIC • ITALIAN* $$

Most of the tables in this cozy, family-run Tuscan restaurant are in view of the wood-fired grill, upon which beef, lamb, and sausages are cooked to perfection. The classic *ribollita* (day-old soup served with bread in the bottom of the bowl) is a winter treat.

 A3 **R5** VIA GERMANICO 58
06-39-72-57-17

INSALATA RICCA *HOT SPOT • ITALIAN* $

This particular location of the restaurant chain is most appreciated for its selection of creative salads and pizzas, which make for a refreshing lunch after a long visit in the Vatican Museums. Try the Rich 6 salad, served in pitalike bread bowl filled with six fresh ingredients.

 A3 **R4** PIAZZA DEL RISORGIMENTO 5/6
06-39-73-03-87

NON SOLO PIZZA *QUICK BITES • PIZZA* $

The main business here is pizza by the slice, but there's also pasta and salads for those looking for something more substantial. Take your food to go, or dine in the no-frills space with a made-to-order meal.

 A3 **R6** VIA DEGLI SCIPIONI 95
06-37-25-820

OLD BRIDGE *QUICK BITES • GELATO* $

The more than 20 homemade varieties are often counted among the best gelato in Rome, but more importantly, they are a treat for people waiting in horrific Vatican Museum lines that wrap around the wall across from Old Bridge. Sadly, though, there's often a line here, too.

MAP **7** A3 **R3** VIALE DEI BASTIONI DI MICHELANGELO 5
06-39-72-30-26

PIERLUIGI   *HOT SPOT • ITALIAN* $$

A table in this ex-pat and Italian-film-industry haunt can be hard
to come by. The simply prepared pastas, meats, and fish are
served in a beautiful outdoor setting, but in colder weather, the
party moves inside to the cozy, low-ceilinged dining room.

 E6 **R**37   PIAZZA DEI RICCI 144
06-68-61-302

SHANTI   *ROMANTIC • INDIAN* $$

With an exotic atmosphere and food to match, Shanti does naan
justice in various flavors like sesame and cheese, and pistachio.
Pair it with curry or tandoori lamb, served alongside a variety
of basmati rice. The lunch menu offers a good selection for just
€8–10 ($10–12).

 A4 **R**8   VIA FABIO MASSIMO 68
06-32-44-922

IL SIMPOSIO DI CONSTANTINI   *QUICK BITES • WINE BAR* $

This upscale wine bar is the perfect place to rest after exploring the Vatican Museums. From the sophisticated menu, try the
house-smoked fish assortment or a cheese course, served with
fresh or dried fruit. Afterwards, take home a bottle from its wine
store next door.

 B6 **R**20   PIAZZA CAVOUR 16
06-32-11-502

LA VERANDA DEL'HOTEL COLUMBUS   *ROMANTIC • ITALIAN* $$$

The city's most stunning outdoor restaurant — with tiki torches
and big, mature trees — features *cucina nuova,* light versions of
Italian classics. Servers are unobtrusive and efficient so that noth-
ing gets in the way of a romantic evening.

 C4 **R**26   BORGO SANTO SPIRITO 73
06-68-72-973

OVERVIEW MAP AND OFF MAP

CHECCHINO DAL 1887   *ROMANTIC • ITALIAN/ROMAN* $$$

Serious Roman cooking can be found in this Monte Testaccio
perch. *Pajate* (intestines), *zampette* (pig's feet), and *coratella*
(heart of beef) are all standard menu items, but there's also pasta
and more common meat dishes, like stewed lamb, for the less
adventurous.

OVERVIEW MAP F3   VIA DI MONTE TESTACCIO 30
06-57-46-318

LA PERGOLA   *ROMANTIC • INTERNATIONAL* $$$

Heinz Beck's restaurant at the Cavalieri Hilton is still Rome's top
culinary destination. Small, exquisite dishes with an eye toward
presentation come with a gorgeous view of the Eternal City. The
international, Mediterranean-influenced menu includes adventures in fish, duck, lamb, and pasta creations.

OFF MAP   VIA ALBERTO CADLOLO 101
06-35-09-22-11

NIGHTLIFE

Hottest club of the moment: **ART CAFÉ**, p. 41

Best place to impress a date: **FLUID**, p. 40

Best café/bar: **ANTICO CAFFÈ DELLA PACE**, p. 40

Best place to christen a new Dolce & Gabbana shirt:
SUPPER CLUB, p. 40

Best beer on tap: **STARBESS ROME BREWING CO.**, p. 45

Best piazza scene: **TAVERNA DEL CAMPO**, p. 40

Best mojito: **FRIEND'S**, p. 43

MAP 1 GHETTO/CAMPO DEI FIORI

SUPPER CLUB *LOUNGE/DANCE CLUB*

An exclusive club hidden within ancient alleys, Supper Club caters to an older professional clientele. When you're not grooving on the dance floor, make yourself comfortable on the beds and beanbags in the lounge.

 A4 3   VIA DEI NARI 14
06-68-80-72-07

TAVERNA DEL CAMPO *BAR*

This no-frills bar serves up reasonably priced drinks to a diverse crowd of locals and visitors. Grab a seat at one of the many outdoor tables and enjoy everything the piazza has to offer.

 C1 18   PIAZZA CAMPO DEI FIORI 16
06-68-74-402

MAP 2 PIAZZA NAVONA/PANTHEON

ANIMA *BAR*

The racy decor at this recently refurbished funky cocktail bar includes velvet couches, beds, and tires. Resident DJs spin acid jazz and drum 'n' bass while the place fills up to the point where you're practically sitting on someone's lap.

 B2 21   VIA SANTA MARIA DELL'ANIMA 57
06-68-64-021

ANTICO CAFFÈ DELLA PACE *BAR*

Eclectic crowds, exceptional wines, and a vintage decor are the fare at this landmark bohemian hangout. The outdoor tables are close together, but the night sky softens the acoustics.

 B1 18   VIA DELLA PACE 4
06-68-61-216

BAR DEL FICO *BAR*

Sit at a table surrounding the central fig *(fico)* tree, and enjoy a drink in one of the loveliest outdoor settings in Rome. The art and photo exhibits add to the aesthetic atmosphere.

 B1 17   PIAZZA DEL FICO 27
06-68-65-205

FLUID *LOUNGE*

Gaze at the lava-lamp walls and stainless steel furnishings while you sip bubbly *prosecco* and nibble on croquettes. The romantic lounge seating and amicable staff will make you feel right at home.

 C1 38   VIA DEL GOVERNO VECCHIO 46
06-68-32-361

JONATHAN'S ANGELS *BAR*

Dressed up in loud colors, theme decorations, and contemporary

THE WHITE NIGHT

If you happen to be in Italy around the end of September, try to get to Rome for the Notte Bianca (White Night). Your mere presence will put you right in the middle of the action as most of the city turns into a gigantic all-night block party. Shops, museums, cinemas, bars, restaurants, outdoor markets, and bars stay open all night and through the morning. When else can you visit a museum at 3 AM and eat pasta and drink wine in a packed restaurant afterwards? It is definitely one of the most unique urban festivals in the world (although other cities, notably Paris, are following Rome's lead), but it only happens one night a year and the date varies from year to year. Find out more at www.lanottebianca.it.

paintings, Jonathan's Angels boasts a decor as vivid as its animated atmosphere. Drop a coin in the bathroom fountain for good luck.

 VIA DELLA FOSSA 16
06-68-93-426

IL LOCALE *LIVE MUSIC*

Performing at Il Locale is what many local bands would consider their big break. Featuring only original music, this small club is packed to capacity – and sometimes beyond – every night.

 VICOLO DEL FICO 3
06-68-89-29-85

MAP 3 TRIDENTE

ART CAFÉ *DANCE CLUB*

This sprawling complex in the Villa Borghese Park Mall boasts an art gallery, live theatrical performances, and a disco. The crowd is mostly under 30 and the festivities move entirely outdoors during the summer.

 VIALE DEL GALOPPATOIO 33
06-36-00-65-78

GILDA *LOUNGE/DANCE CLUB*

This chic piano bar is a quiet after-hours alternative to Rome's club scene. Pricey cocktails, wine by the glass, and separate disco-and-dancing space draw a middle-aged clientele.

 VIA MARIO DEI FIORI 97
06-67-84-838

STRAVINSKIJ BAR AT HOTEL DE RUSSIE *BAR*

Being an overnight guest is not a prerequisite to sipping champagne with the after-dinner pack at this classy hotel bar. The brilliantly designed lounge seating is nap-inducingly comfortable.

 A3 5 VIA DEL BABUINO 9
06-32-88-81

MAP 4 | VIA VENETO/TERMINI

HARRY'S BAR *BAR*

Named after the Venetian original, this elegant, expensive bar and restaurant hosts the Via Veneto set. Sip a Bellini while listening to the lovely piano music.

 B2 4 VIA VENETO 150
06-47-42-103

HOTEL EDEN *BAR*

Adjacent to the excellent La Terrazza restaurant, this bar has the same panoramic view of Rome for only the price of a cocktail. Patrons are treated to nightly piano music and fine service as well.

 C1 5 VIA LUDOVISI 49
06-47-81-21

JACKIE O. *PIANO BAR/DANCE CLUB*

As elegant as the former first lady herself, this space is often rented out for private functions. When it's open, you'll find a disco and piano bar filled with a thirtysomething crowd dressed to impress. Reservations recommended on weekends.

 C2 10 VIA BONCOMPAGNI 11
06-42-88-54-57

MAP 5 | COLOSSEO

COMING OUT PUB *QUEER*

All are welcomed at this predominantly gay and lesbian pub in Rome's unofficial queer district. The very pubby interior and live music on weekends make for a relaxed setting to toss back a few.

 D4 37 VIA DI SAN GIOVANNI IN LATERANO 8
06-70-09-871

FINNEGAN'S IRISH PUB *PUB*

Out of the several Irish pubs in Rome, Finnegan's claims to be the only one that's actually Irish owned. Regardless, the relaxed and friendly ambience makes it the perfect place to enjoy a pint of Guinness.

 C3 25 VIA LEONINA 66
06-47-47-026

BIG MAMA   CHAKRA CAFÉ

HANGAR   *QUEER*

An institution of the Rome gay scene, this American-owned bar is known to get crazy on weekends. Men of all ages are the majority here, but women are also welcome.

 MAP 5 C4 **Ⓝ27**   VIA IN SELCI 69
06-48-81-39-71

THE LUX   *DANCE CLUB*

Much more low-key in the early evening, this gay-friendly club hosts a crowd of primarily 25–35-year-olds. There are several rooms to choose from and the dance floor explodes after midnight.

 MAP 5 B2 **Ⓝ10**   SALITA DEL GRILLO 7
06-67-81-799

MAP 6 TRASTEVERE

BIG MAMA   *JAZZ CLUB*

A highly regarded blues and jazz club, this tiny Trastevere haunt also offers R&B and African music. If you plan to see more than one show, opt for the well-priced annual membership.

 MAP 6 D3 **Ⓝ25**   VICOLO SAN FRANCESCO A RIPA 18
06-58-12-551

CHAKRA CAFÉ   *LOUNGE*

The cocktails are mixed to perfection at this discreet, Asian-themed outpost. There is also an ample selection of wines, herbal teas, and fresh desserts.

 MAP 6 B3 **Ⓝ17**   PIAZZA DI SANTA RUFINA 13
06-58-16-649

FRIEND'S   *BAR*

Mojito-sipping twenty- and thirtysomethings flock to this trendy bar after dinner and usually wind up making a night of it. Outdoor tables double as front row seating for street performers in the adjacent piazza.

 MAP 6 A2 **Ⓝ5**   PIAZZA TRILUSSA 34
06-58-16-111

MONTE TESTACCIO

Monte Testaccio wasn't always the stomping ground of Rome's hip and beautiful. This southernmost hill of Rome's historical working-class quarter is supposedly the fossilized remnants of what was once the city's ancient garbage dump. Today, however, its nightlife scene is hard to top. The area's rush hour starts after midnight when Romans of all ages fill the several nocturnal haunts lining Via di Monte Testaccio. The dance floor at the predominantly gay **Alibi (p. 45)** brings together the scantily clad and gorgeous until the wee hours. A slightly more subdued scene prevails at **Zoo Bar (p. 45)** where live rock bands and DJs rock the house until after 3 AM. Those seeking something a bit more upscale, yet not lacking in terms of energy, head to **Caffè Latino (p. 45).**

LETTERE CAFFÉ *LIVE MUSIC*
This literary café and performance space is the first of its kind in Rome. Local and international musicians and poets perform nightly in a tranquil, almost library-like atmosphere.

 D3 **26** VIA DI SAN FRANCESCO A RIPA 100/101
06-58-33-43-79

STARDUST *BAR*
A relaxed atmosphere complemented by cozy couches and an abundance of candles lure patrons of all ages to this Trastevere institution.

 A2 **10** VICOLO DEI RENZI 4
06-58-32-08-75

MAP **7** VATICANO

FONCLEA *LIVE MUSIC*
Filled with couples and fevered intellectuals, this cavelike cellar provides an an authentic pub atmosphere with the added bonus of live music, often jazz, R&B, and Latin tunes.

MAP **7** **B4** **17** VIA CRESCENZIO 82
06-68-96-302

NUVOLARI *WINE BAR*
A rarity in this sleepy ancient quarter known as Borgo, this stylish wine bar is an ideal place for a pre-dinner aperitif or a quiet night out with your significant other.

MAP **7** **B4** **19** VIA DEGLI OMBRELLARI 10
06-68-80-30-18

LETTERE CAFFÉ

STARDUST

OVERVIEW MAP

ALEXANDERPLATZ *JAZZ CLUB*
Possibly the city's most respected jazz club, Alexanderplatz spotlights famous musicians from Europe and the United States. The shows move outdoors to Villa Celimontana during the summer.

OVERVIEW MAP B1 VIA OSTIA 9
06-39-74-21-71

ALIBI *DANCE CLUB*
Among Rome's most noteworthy gay bars, Alibi opens its wonderful roof garden in the summer and plays disco and alternative music on its high-tech sound system year-round. The expensive cover includes your first drink.

OVERVIEW MAP F3 VIA DI MONTE TESTACCIO 44
06-57-43-448

CAFFÈ LATINO *DANCE CLUB*
The hub of Rome's Latin music scene, Caffè Latino features three distinct spaces for its stylish, late-night crowd: an upscale bar, a stage for live concerts, and a quieter room that screens music videos.

OVERVIEW MAP F3 VIA DI MONTE TESTACCIO 96
06-57-28-85-56

STARBESS ROME BREWING CO. *PUB*
With its long tables and wood-panel booths, this Roman microbrew pub seems like it belongs in Germany. A variety of tasty ales and lagers are on tap, with Italian pub grub to accompany them.

OVERVIEW MAP B1 VIA PASSAGLIA 1
06-39-72-11-53

ZOO BAR *DANCE CLUB*
More subdued than its clubby neighbors, this ultracasual space has a café atmosphere and a dance floor in the back. DJs or occasional live acts generate blues, rock, and danceable tunes for Zoo Bar's friendly patrons.

OVERVIEW MAP F3 VIA DI MONTE TESTACCIO 22
339-27-27-995

S SHOPS

Best place to shop like a paparazzi star: **ELEONORA**, p. 53

Best place for unique gifts:
MERCATO DI PORTA PORTESE, p. 59

Best "only in Rome" buy: **FORNARI**, p. 54

Most tempting gourmet store: **I SOLITI IGNOTI**, p. 52

Best shopping for him: **SERMONETA TIES**, p. 56

Best shopping for her: **TAD**, p. 56

Best souvenir shopping: **NARDECCHIA**, p. 51

Where to shop like a Rome insider: **LEONE LIMENTANI**, p. 48

Best quality leather: **MEROLA**, p. 55

MAP 1 GHETTO/CAMPO DEI FIORI

AMORE E PSICHE *BOOKS*

Specializing in psychology, arts, and humanities books, this small but densely packed store also stocks a good selection of classics in English.

MAP 1 A5 **S**4 VIA DI SANTA CATERINA DA SIENA 61
06-67-83-908

ANTICA ERBORISTERIA *BATH AND BEAUTY*

Featuring both prepackaged and made-to-order herbal remedies, the quaint Antica Erboristeria also sells antique pharmaceutical supplies, handmade paper, and licorice. Shopkeepers are all trained herbalists.

MAP 1 B4 **S**15 VIA DI TORRE ARGENTINA 15
06-68-79-493

BEST SELLER *CLOTHING AND SHOES*

On one of the best shopping streets near Campo dei Fiori, you'll find prêt-a-porter lines from all the famous designers, including Dolce & Gabbana, at great prices.

MAP 1 C2 **S**25 VIA DEI GIUBBONARI 96
06-68-13-60-40

CAMPO DEI FIORI

See SIGHTS, p. 2.

MAP 1 C2 **O**21 PIAZZA CAMPO DEI FIORI

CONFETTERIA MORIONDO E GARIGLIO *GOURMET GOODIES*

This family-run chocolate maker specializes in holiday sweets – there's always a line out the door on Valentine's Day. The shop will also deliver to hotels within Rome.

MAP 1 A6 **S**5 VIA PIÈ DI MARMO 21/22
06-69-90-856

LEONE LIMENTANI *GIFT AND HOME*

This labyrinthine warehouse of china, flatware, and cookery would make Martha Stewart swoon. For missing china, wedding gifts, original Italian ceramics and silver, this is the place to find it.

MAP 1 E5 **S**36 VIA DEL PORTICO D'OTTAVIA 47
06-68-80-69-49

MONDELLO OTTICA *ACCESSORIES*

Mondello Ottica focuses on designer eyewear from the likes of Fendi, Gucci, and Armani, carrying both sunglasses and frames for prescriptions. They'll make adjustments and minor repairs for free.

MAP 1 B1 **S**7 VIA DEL PELLEGRINO 98
06-68-61-955

PINKO *CLOTHING AND SHOES*

This location of the trendy Italian chain stocks the best in model-worthy fashion, with two floors of the latest looks and accessories like their own line of canvas bags.

MAP 1 C2 **S**22 VIA DEI GIUBBONARI 76-77
06-68-30-94-46

ANTICA ERBORISTERIA   MONDELLO OTTICA

RACHELE *KIDS STUFF*
Purveying the finest clothing for children, Rachele only carries
handmade togs for infants to seven-year-olds. Special orders for
older children (up to age 12) can be made upon request.

 B1 ⑤6   VICOLO DEL BOLLO 7
06-68-64-975

RINASCITA *BOOKS AND MUSIC*
The ground-floor bookstore carries mainstream novels in English,
and the basement music collection holds mostly European and
U.S. new releases, along with a compelling selection of world-
music, especially from Latin America.

 C6 ⑤30   VIA DELLE BOTTEGHE OSCURE 1
06-67-97-637

SPAZIO SETTE *GIFT AND HOME*
A huge 17th-century palace houses this collection of mostly 20th-
and 21st-century furniture. Don't worry about fitting your purchase on the plane – Spazio Sette will ship anywhere.

 C4 ⑤26   VIA DEI BARBIERI 7
06-68-69-747

MAP 2 PIAZZA NAVONA/PANTHEON

AI MONASTERI *GOURMET GOODIES*
Gourmets revere Ai Monasteri's liqueurs, jams, chocolates, and
other foodstuffs, which are all handmade by Cistercian monks
from various Italian monasteries.

 B3 ⑤25   CORSO RINASCIMENTO 72
06-68-80-27-83

ART DECO GALLERY *GIFT AND HOME*
With its selection of furniture, vases, and lighting, this gallery
presents an eclectic collection of original French, Italian, and
Austrian home accessories from the 1920s and '30s.

 A2 ⑤7   VIA DEI CORONARI 14
06-67-86-241

BERTÉ   IL PAPIRO

ARTE *GIFT AND HOME*
Form and function unite at this beautiful showcase of contemporary design. Everything – from blenders to dish racks – is assessed for quality as well as aesthetic beauty.

 B4 **$28** PIAZZA RONDANINI 32
06-68-33-907

BERTÉ *KIDS STUFF*
Berté is Rome's grandest toy store. Its display window, which often showcases doll collections or oversized stuffed animals, is a delightful distraction for the many strollers on ever-crowded Piazza Navona.

 C3 **$41** PIAZZA NAVONA 107–111
06-68-75-011

LA CITTÀ DEL SOLE *KIDS STUFF*
This densely packed and hard-to-navigate store specializes in politically correct educational toys. Luckily, the staff knows where everything is and will help you find what you're looking for.

 A3 **$9** VIA DELLA SCROFA 65
06-68-80-38-05

DEGLI EFFETTI *CLOTHING AND SHOES*
This trio of boutiques is perhaps the most expensive clothing store outside the Tridente area. You'll find the latest creations from Japanese designers, as well as labels like Helmut Lang.

 B5 **$34** PIAZZA CAPRANICA 75, 79, 93
06-67-90-202

LIBRERIA HERDER *BOOKS*
The dense shelves of this used bookstore – one of Rome's best – often yield obscure texts for the diligent browsers. The friendly staff will happily help you search for titles among the stock of primarily German, French, and English texts.

 A5 **$14** PIAZZA DI MONTECITORIO 117-120
06-67-94-628

MAGA MORGANA *CLOTHING AND SHOES*
This store duo – one selling new frocks, the other vintage – is a treasure trove of vintage, unique, and limited-edition women's

DOLLAR-FRIENDLY SHOPPING

The halcyon days of the low-valued lira are over, and the high value of the euro over the dollar has made finding great deals in Italy increasingly difficult. But it's not impossible. Bargain-savvy Romans head to street markets like **Mercato di Porta Portese (p. 59)** and in **Campo dei Fiori (p. 2)** to troll for clothing, jewelry, and art — both vintage and new — at good and negotiable prices. Frugal fashionistas hit **Discount dell'Alta Moda (p. 53)** and the **Tad (p. 56)** outlet store for drastic drops on high fashion prices. But the biggest deals come twice a year. From mid-July to mid-September and mid-December to early March, all stores are required to hold sales, slashing prices by 50–80 percent. Romans wait all year to swarm **Via Condotti (p. 57),** where staggering discounts can even be found in luxury shops like Gucci, Prada, Armani, and Versace.

fashion, which includes suede, leather, and faux-fur coats, plus wedding gowns and one-of-a-kind vegetable-dyed knits.

 VIA DEL GOVERNO VECCHIO 27-29
06-68-79-995

NARDECCHIA *VINTAGE AND ANTIQUES*
Stop in this well-respected Piazza Navona gallery to admire its famous black-and-white prints of the city. Prices to buy range from affordable to very expensive.

 PIAZZA NAVONA 25
06-68-69-318

ORNAMENTUM *GIFT AND HOME*
The specialty of this fabric house — worth a visit just to gawk — is its luxurious silks for the home in every imaginable color. The store will ship anywhere.

 VIA DEI CORONARI 227
06-68-76-849

IL PAPIRO *GIFT AND HOME*
Find stationery for both everyday and extraordinary occasions at this pretty shop. Most of the papers are made by hand, and there are calligraphy supplies as well.

 VIA DEL PANTHEON 50
06-67-95-597

QUADRIFOGLIO OUTLET *KIDS STUFF*
An upscale kids' boutique, Quadrifoglio concentrates on adorable,

handmade clothing for kids 0-10. Instead of having August sales, this shop keeps its prices low year-round.

 B4 **S29** VIA DELLE COLONNELLE 10
06-67-84-917

I SOLITI IGNOTI *GOURMET GOODIES*
Specializing in gourmet foods from every Italian region, I Soliti Ignoti stocks a tantalizing selection of edibles, including wines, spices, salamis, and hard-to-find cheeses. Small groups can dine on-site by appointment.

 B2 **S24** VIA DEL TEATRO PACE 37
06-68-89-12-60

TANCA *VINTAGE AND ANTIQUES*
Old photographic prints, heirloom jewelry, and estate silver are some of the disparate relics you'll find at this cluttered, but very welcoming, shop.

 B3 **S27** SALITA DE CRESCENZI 12
06-68-75-272

VIA DEI CORONARI *SHOPPING DISTRICT*
Antique furniture, art, jewelry, and more abound in the more than 40 stores that lie along this narrow, cobblestoned street that is Rome's official antiques district.

 A1 **S2** VIA DEI CORONARI BTWN. VIA ZANARDELLI AND PIAZZA DEI
CORONARI

MAP 3 | TRIDENTE

ALINARI *GIFT AND HOME*
The Alinari family's original black-and-white photographs of Italian cities are the focus of their shop, open since the 1800s.

 C4 **S24** VIA ALIBERT 16A
06-67-92-923

ANGLO-AMERICAN BOOK CO. *BOOKS AND MUSIC*
A lifeline to English-language books and textbooks for expats and students in Rome, Anglo-American carries U.S. and British titles. Their packed shelves of fiction, nonfiction, and art books make for great browsing.

 E5 **S58** VIA DELLA VITE 102
06-67-95-222

AVC BY ADRIANA CAMPANILE *ACCESSORIES AND SHOES*
Classic Italian shoes and handbags are the only things on the menu at this lovely boutique responsible for outfitting Romans and visitors of all levels of fame.

 C4 **S27** PIAZZA DI SPAGNA 88/89
06-67-80-095

BATTISTONI *CLOTHING AND SHOES*
A well-established clothing store for both men and women, Battistoni designs its own suits, shirts, shoes, and accessories.

ANGLO-AMERICAN BOOK CO.   AVC BY ADRIANA CAMPANILE

Politicians like the conservative, sophisticated styles, and the Via Condotti address ensures quality.

 MAP 3 D4 **S** 37   VIA CONDOTTI 61A
06-67-86-827

BOTTEGA VENETA   *ACCESSORIES*

Elegantly displaying their signature butter-soft leather goods, this luxury Italian chain store sells men's and women's accessories and fashion in classic looks with a modern flair.

 MAP 3 E3 **S** 56   PIAZZA SAN LORENZO IN LUCINA 9
06-68-21-00-24

BUCCONE   *GOURMET GOODIES*

Part candy store, part wine shop, and part café, Buccone has been in business since 1870. The attentive staff will present even the smallest purchase with style.

 MAP 3 B2 **S** 7   VIA DI RIPETTA 19
06-36-12-154

DISCOUNT DELL' ALTA MODA   *CLOTHING AND SHOES*

Haute-couture, designer suits, and accessories from brands like Armani and Zegna are all marked at 40–50 percent off. The racks of fashion for him and her include irregulars and overstock at temptingly low price tags.

 MAP 3 B3 **S** 12   VIA DI GESÙ E MARIA 16A
06-36-13-796

ELEONORA   *CLOTHING AND SHOES*

The owner handpicks the high-fashion, sexy clothes that fill this shop. Find yourself dizzy from all the Gucci, YSL, and Galliano? Relax in the exclusive VIP dressing room complete with a fully stocked bar.

 MAP 3 C4 **S** 26   VIA DEL BABUINO 97
06-67-93-173

ENRICO CAMPONI   *VINTAGE AND ANTIQUES*

If you can't get to Venice, Enrico Camponi is the place in Rome to buy Murano glass. Many of these colorful pieces, including some beautiful vases, are Venini antiques.

 MAP 3 F2 **S** 66   VIA DELLA STELLETTA 32
06-68-65-249

FAUSTO SANTINI   FEMME SISTINA

FARMACIA PESCI   *BATH AND BEAUTY*
In business since the 16th century, the oldest pharmacy in the
Eternal City offers contemporary services (like prescription
refills), as well as consultations on herbal and homeopathic remedies.

 F5❺72   PIAZZA DI TREVI 89
06-67-92-210

FAUSTO SANTINI   *ACCESSORIES AND SHOES*
This whimsical shoe and handbag designer has a loyal following
of customers in the arts. His line changes yearly, but the products
are consistent in their cutting-edge quality.

 D4❺40   VIA FRATTINA 120
06-67-84-114

FEMME SISTINA   *BATH AND BEAUTY*
Pamper yourself with a visit to this old-guard salon whose styl-
ists have worked on celebrities like Audrey Hepburn and Nicole
Kidman. The hair, skin, and nail services are all worthy splurges.

 D5❺46   VIA SISTINA 75A
06-67-80-260

FORNARI   *GIFT AND HOME*
Since 1905, Fornari has been building its reputation for the most
beautiful handcrafted sterling silver, china, and crystal. Available
only in Italy, these goods make special wedding gifts.

 D4❺41   VIA FRATTINA 133
06-67-80-105

FRANCESCO BIASIA   *ACCESSORIES*
Among the most innovative handbag designers in the world,
Biasia uses high-tech fabrics and traditional animal skins to create
unique purses and wallets of exceptional quality.

 D5❺49   VIA DUE MACELLI 62
06-67-92-727

FRETTE   *GIFT AND HOME*
The world's most famous linen store, Frette – with its luxurious,
elegant styles – is a thread-counter's dream and has prices to
match. August sales bring mark downs of up to 50 percent.

 F4❺68   VIA DEL CORSO 381
06-67-86-862

GALLERIA ALBERTO SORDI *SHOPPING CENTER*
This is the closest thing to a mall in Rome, and it's filled with original and chain shops such as Zara, Pianegonda, Jam, Calvin Klein, and the Italian bookstore/café chain La Feltrinelli.

MAP 3 **F4 S 70** PIAZZA COLONNA 31/35

GIOIELLI IN MOVIMENTO *JEWELRY*
Featuring items like rings with changeable stones, the unique jewelry designs here double as works of art, with the prices that would suggest. You can also custom design your own masterpiece.

MAP 3 **F2 S 67** VIA DELLA STELLETTA 23
06-68-67-431

GUSTO E SALUTE *GOURMET GOODIES*
If your gourmet taste buds are sensitive to allergies or prefer natural treats, head here for fresh and packaged baked goods, savory snacks, organic wines, and dried pastas.

MAP 3 **F6 S 74** VIA DELLA PANETTERIA 8
06-67-96-259

H. MARTINELLI *JEWELRY*
The Roman branch of this family-run mini-empire is the place to go for that once-in-a-lifetime purchase of art deco-influenced jewelry.

MAP 3 **D4 S 35** VIA MARIO DEI FIORI 59B
06-67-97-733

THE LION BOOKSHOP *BOOKS*
With a stock of fiction and nonfiction titles in English, as well as a reading room and café service, this cozy spot provides respite from the throngs of shoppers outside.

MAP 3 **C3 S 22** VIA DEI GRECI 33
06-32-65-40-07

MARIELLA BURANI *CLOTHING AND SHOES*
This designer's Tridente shop showcases both her haute couture and her ready-to-wear creations. The choices in the small space range from loud and playful to more formal eveningwear.

MAP 3 **D4 S 34** VIA BOCCA DI LEONE 28
06-67-90-630

MEROLA *ACCESSORIES*
Open by appointment only, Europe's oldest glove store has fitted the hands of Hollywood and real-life royalty in custom leather and cloth gloves since 1885. Audrey Hepburn wore a pair in *Roman Holiday*.

MAP 3 **B3 S 11** VIA DEL CORSO 143
06-67-91-961

IL MESSAGERIE *BOOKS AND MUSIC*
With two floors of international CDs, books, magazines, and DVDs, including a wide selection of Italian regional music, Il Messagerie is the best-stocked music store in the city.

MAP 3 **C3 S 21** VIA DEL CORSO 473
06-68-44-01

L'OLFATTORIA BAR A PARFUMS *BATH AND BEAUTY*
Find hundreds of French fragrances, candles, and essential oils to sample, sniff, and appreciate at this "perfume bar." You can also create individual scents with the help of the shop's olfactory experts.

 MAP 3 B2 **⑤8** VIA DI RIPETTA 34
06-36-12-325

PINEIDER *GIFT AND HOME*
Find the perfect gift for a recent college graduate or a new executive among Pineider's exclusive handmade Florentine leather desk accessories. The custom services include invitations and engraving.

 MAP 3 D3 **⑤32** VIA DELLA FONTANELLA BORGHESE 22
06-68-78-369

PROFUMERIA MATEROZZOLI *BATH AND BEAUTY*
In business since 1870, this perfume store stocks all the major brands, plus some rare ones, like Acqua di Parma. For men, there are quality shaving accessories, too.

 MAP 3 E3 **⑤57** PIAZZA SAN LORENZO IN LUCINA 5
06-68-89-26-86

RIZZOLI *BOOKS AND MUSIC*
The Rome location of this sophisticated bookstore chain stocks art volumes by internationally acclaimed Italian painters and photographers, along with a nice selection of English-language books for the cultured reader.

 MAP 3 F4 **⑤69** LARGO CHIGI 15
06-67-96-641

SERMONETA TIES *ACCESSORIES*
The cravat-savvy know Sermoneta for its variety, high quality, and reasonable prices. Original ties by owner Giorgio Sermonata are sold alongside such labels as Armani, Versace, and Fendi.

 MAP 3 D4 **⑤36** VIA MARIO DEI FIORI 37
06-67-90-106

TAD *GIFT AND HOME*
If it's hip, it's here at Tad, Rome's answer to Barneys. The clothing, accessories, home decor, and beauty products all show an eye for design and luxury. There's also an outlet with prices slashed up to 70 percent on out-of-season goods.

 MAP 3 B3 **⑤14** VIA DEL BABUINO 155A
06-32-69-51-29

TESTA *CLOTHING AND SHOES*
This men's clothing store designs one-of-a-kind pieces and also hawks other designer lines at a considerable discount. Suits, in particular, are a bargain compared to other boutiques.

 MAP 3 D5 **⑤47** VIA BORGOGNONA 13
06-67-91-296

VALENTINO *CLOTHING AND SHOES*
Not far from the fashion icon's palatial Roman headquarters, this salon of haute couture showcases Valentino's romantic and

elegant mens- and womenswear, each housed in separate in-store boutiques.

 D4 **S** 38   VIA BOCCA DI LEONE 15
06-67-83-656

VIA CONDOTTI/VIA DEL CORSO *SHOPPING DISTRICT*
The Rodeo Drive of Rome intersects with Tridente's main and mainstream shopping avenue: Find high fashion on Condotti and trendy shops on Corso, making this area a shopper's heaven.

 D3 **S** 33   VIA CONDOTTI BTWN. VIA DEL CORSO AND PIAZZA DI
SPAGNA; VIA DEL CORSO BTWN. PIAZZA DEL POPOLO AND
PIAZZA VENEZIA

MAP 4 VIA VENETO/TERMINI

ENHANCEMENTS UNIQUE NAIL SPA *BATH, BEAUTY, AND SPA*
Rome's first nail spa, this posh yet serene space offers original mani/pedi treatments using its own line of luxurious products. You can also sip espresso or champagne while being pampered.

 C2 **S** 12   VIA UMBRIA 13
06-42-01-34-96

ESIA BOOKS AND JOURNALS *BOOKS*
Popular with college students from La Sapienza, this bookshop carries the best English-language selection of academic texts in northern Rome, as well as a number of literary journals.

 D5 **S** 28   VIA PALESTRO 30
06-44-63-505

FELTRINELLI INTERNATIONAL *BOOKS AND MUSIC*
Feltrinelli is Italy's version of Barnes and Noble. This outpost carries Rome's best selection of English-language travel guides. Fiction and nonfiction titles, CDs, and original-language DVDs complete the global offerings.

 D3 **S** 22   VIA VITTORIO EMANUELE ORLANDO 84
06-48-27-878

TRIMANI *GOURMET GOODIES*
The shelves of this wine shop-cum-gourmet food store hold such delicacies as truffle paste and dried porcini mushrooms, as well as exquisite olive oils that you can taste before you buy.

 C4 **S** 16   VIA GOITO 20
06-44-69-661

UPIM *CLOTHING AND SHOES*
If you've forgotten anything for your trip, stop by Upim for the unbelievably low prices on swimsuits, underwear, clothing, cosmetics, toiletries, toys, and luggage. There are branches throughout the city, but this one is conveniently located near Termini train station.

 F4 **S** 40   VIA GIOBERTI 64
06-44-65-579

LE GALLINELLE *CLOTHING*
In this funky former butcher shop, marble slabs that once held meat now display vintage clothes and vintage-inspired designs for men and women.

 B3 **⑬** VIA DEL BOSCHETTO 76
06-48-81-017

IL GIARDINO DEL TÈ *GOURMET GOODIES*
In a coffee-centric city, this tea boutique in the funky Monti neighborhood is a testament to the trend of tea drinking. Find varieties of black, green, and white teas from India, China, and Japan, as well as original tea sets on offer.

 B3 **⑯** VIA DEL BOSCHETTO 112A
06-47-46-888

RICORDI *MUSIC*
Stocking CDs from the world over, this large store keeps a particularly good selection of vintage Italian music from all 20 regions, especially Naples.

 B1 **⑦** VIA CESARE BATTISTI 120
06-67-98-022

MAP 6 TRASTEVERE

THE ALMOST CORNER BOOKSHOP *BOOKS*
Its diverse selection of English books, personal service, and fair prices make this shop an expat favorite. Something not in stock? The staff will order in titles for you with rush delivery when possible.

 A2 **⑨** VIA DEL MORO 45
06-58-36-942

BIBLI *BOOKS AND MUSIC*
Bibli's café is as big a draw as the books, which include a selection of English-language novels. There's also a stage for live musical performances and computers for web surfing.

 C3 **㉑** VIA DEI FIENAROLI 28
06-58-84-097

INNOCENZI *GOURMET GOODIES*
An international food store, Innocenzi carries imported products of all kinds, especially those from neighboring Mediterranean countries, such as Greek olive oil.

 C2 **⑳** PIAZZA SAN COSIMATO 66
06-58-12-725

LABORATORIO ARTI DECORATIVE *ACCESSORIES AND JEWELRY*
Watch the owners at work in this small studio/shop making delicate, colorful things in glass and stone,

RICORDI   SCALA QUATTORDICI

including jewelry and home accessories. Commission a piece, and they'll send it to you in two weeks.

 MAP 6 A2 **S** 7   VICOLO DEL CINQUE 13
06-58-13-317

MERCATO DI PORTA PORTESE *GIFT AND HOME*
Taking over Porta Portese every Sunday morning, Rome's largest and most famous flea market is a sprawling bustle of vintage clothing, furniture, books, and home accessories. Be sure to bargain.

 MAP 6 E3 **S** 28   PIAZZA DI PORTA PORTESE

OFFICINA DELLA CARTA *GIFT AND HOME*
This old-world custom stationer sells handmade invitations, business cards, announcements, and more. The staff will work with you to design your pieces and help navigate the range of aesthetic options.

 MAP 6 A2 **S** 2   VIA BENEDETTA 26B
06-58-95-557

SCALA QUATTORDICI *CLOTHING*
Scala Quattordici sells off-the-rack silk clothing for women, but also makes items to order in surprisingly little time. Among the accessories, the richly colored scarves are excellent gifts.

 MAP 6 B2 **S** 11   VIA DELLA SCALA 13
06-58-83-580

SHARM *ACCESSORIES AND JEWELRY*
Beads, rocks, ribbons, and shells adorn eye-catching and original bags and jewelry at this family-run store. The eclectic, one-of-a-kind designs are moderately priced for such beautiful and high-quality goods.

 MAP 6 A2 **S** 6   VIA DELLA SCALA 70
06-58-33-44-77

MAP 7 | VATICANO

CARLO GIUNTA *VINTAGE AND ANTIQUES*
This well-designed shop sparingly displays its wares, which include

antique ceramic objects from all over Italy and contemporary Sicilian tableware known for featuring bright, playful colors.

 D6 **S**31 VIA DEI CORONARI 83/84
06-68-64-192

CASTRONI *GOURMET GOODIES*
A haven for homesick U.S. tourists craving peanut butter and Rice Krispies, Castroni stocks foodstuffs from around the world, including an international coffee-bean selection at the in-store bar.

 A5 **S**9 VIA COLA DI RIENZO 196
06-68-74-383

MONDADORI *BOOKS AND MUSIC*
This well-stocked Vatican-area bookshop also sells CDs, DVDs, and literary gift items like reading accessories. The service is cordial, and some sales associates speak English.

 A6 **S**10 PIAZZA COLA DI RIENZO 81
06-32-20-188

SAVELLI ARTE E TRADIZIONE *GIFT AND HOME*
Descandants of popes, the Savellis have made secular and religious art since 1898. They are famous for their mosaics, but their goods range from small pieces like crucifixes and calendars to larger items like ceramic nativity sets.

 C3 **S**24 VIA PAOLO VI 29
06-68-30-70-17

LA SINOPIA *VINTAGE AND ANTIQUES*
Antique experts staff this highly respected shop, which mostly sells furniture from the 18th and 19th centuries. They also consult on restoration and care of your valuable purchases.

 E6 **S**36 VIA DEI BANCHI VECCHI 21C
06-68-72-869

VIA COLA DI RIENZO *SHOPPING DISTRICT*
Fashionable stores for men, women and children line this main Vaticano drag where unique Italian stores like kidswear favorite Iana share the blocks with such international chains as Benetton.

 A4 **S**7 VIA COLA DI RIENZO BTWN. PIAZZA DEL RISORGIMENTO AND
THE TIBER RIVER

OVERVIEW MAP

VOLPETTI *GOURMET GOODIES*
Volpetti is the best cheese store in Rome. Rinds of hand-selected, artisanal cheeses from all over Italy are lovingly washed each morning, with products shippable to anywhere in the world.

OVERVIEW MAP E3 VIA MARMORATA 47
06-57-42-352

A ARTS AND LEISURE

MUSEUMS AND GALLERIES

MAP 1 | GHETTO/CAMPO DEI FIORI

ASSOCIAZIONE CULTURALE L'ATTICO
This avant-garde contemporary gallery showcases young, mostly European artists. Many of the paintings, sculptures, and multimedia installations are implicitly political.

 B2 **10**   VIA DEL PARADISO 41
06-68-69-846

GALLERIA SPADA
This 16th-century palazzo contains Rome's best architectural trompe l'oeil, Borromini's arcade. Also on display are the collections are 17th-century art wheeler-dealer, Cardinal Bernardino Spada, who launched the careers of such baroque artists as Guido Reni and Guercino.

 D1 **31**   PIAZZA CAPO DI FERRO 13
06-68-74-896

MUSEO BARRACCO DI SCULTURA ANTICA
Donated to Rome in the early 20th century, Baron Giovanni Barracco's once-private collection of pre-Roman sculptures includes Babylonian stone lions, ancient Greek vases, and fragments of Greek carvings.

 A1 **1**   CORSO VITTORIO EMANUELE II 166
06-68-80-68-48

MUSEO EBRAICO DI ROMA
The city's heavily guarded synagogue houses a museum that documents Rome's Jewish population. Religious ritual objects, 16th-century papal decrees against the Jews, and personal effects from concentration camps are among its treasured artifacts.

 F5 **39**   LUNGOTEVERE DEI CENCI (SINAGOGA)
06-68-40-06-61

MUSEO NAZIONALE ROMANO – CRYPTA BALBI
Discovered in 1981, this archaeological complex opened in 2000. The highlight is the lobby of the ancient (13 BC) Teatro di Balbo, but interpretive space is used throughout the site to explain archaeology and its methods.

 C5 **29**   VIA DELLE BOTTEGHE OSCURE 31
06-39-96-77-00

PALAZZO BRASCHI MUSEO DI ROMA
This museum presents a cultural, social, and artistic view of Rome

MUSEO BARRACCO DI
SCULTURA ANTICA

MUSEO NAZIONALE ROMANO – PALAZZO ALTEMPS

through paintings that depict its spectacular pageants. The architecture of this turn-of-the-19th-century palace is worth a look as well, especially the grand staircase, with its 18 red granite columns.

 A2 **2** PIAZZA DI SAN PANTALEO 10
06-67-10-83-46

MAP 2 | PIAZZA NAVONA/PANTHEON

MUSEO NAZIONALE ROMANO – PALAZZO ALTEMPS
The beautiful 15th-century palazzo is a wonderful place to pass an afternoon amidst intimate courtyards and ancient sculpture, some of which was restored by baroque masters. The palace's theater was restored in 2003 and hosts occasional concerts.

 A2 **6** PIAZZA DI SANT'APOLLINARE 48
06-68-33-566 OR 06-68-48-51

SALA DELL'INSTITUTO CERVANTES
Right on Piazza Navona across from the Four Rivers Fountain, this friendly gallery highlights contemporary artists from Spain and is dependable for good quality.

 B3 **26** PIAZZA NAVONA 91/92
06-85-37-36-01

SANTA MARIA SOPRA MINERVA
Built over the ruins of the Temple of Minerva, this Gothic-style church has a wealth of Renaissance art. Don't miss the Annunciation scene painted in the frescoes (1488-1493) by Fra Filippino Lippi in the Carafa Chapel in the right transept or the marble *Risen Christ* (1519-1521) in the presbytery, which is attributed to Michelangelo.

 C5 **45** PIAZZA DELLA MINERVA 42
06-67-93-926

**MAP 3** TRIDENTE

ACCADEMIA DI FRANCIA VILLA MEDICI
Completed in 1575, this magnificent villa has been the home of the French Academy since 1804, founded by Louis XIV in 1666 to boost the careers of young French artists. The excellent exhibits range in media and time period.

 B5 **15** VIALE DELLA TRINITÀ DEI MONTE 1
06-67-611 OR 06-67-61-311

GALLERIA DELL'ACCADEMIA DI SAN LUCA
Accademia di San Luca, a private arts academy founded in 1577, includes Raphael's beloved painting *Madonna of St. Luke* and other Renaissance works. The museum is scheduled to reopen in late 2006, after extensive renovations.

 E5 **63** PIAZZA DELL'ACCADEMIA DI SAN LUCA 77
06-67-98-850

GALLERIA F. RUSSO
This gallery mounts shows by 20th-century Italian painters and photographers, such as Carlo Erba and De Chirico, with occasional exhibits of international work as well.

 C4 **23** VIA ALIBERT 18
06-67-89-949

MUSEO NAZIONALE DELLE PASTE ALIMENTARI
The guided tours at Rome's only museum devoted to food may provide too much information for the casual visitor, but cooks and food historians will appreciate the attention to minute detail.

 F6 **75** PIAZZA SCANDERBERG 117
06-69-91-120

MAP 4 VIA VENETO/TERMINI

GALLERIA NAZIONALE D'ARTE ANTICA
DI PALAZZO BARBERINI
Located in the Palazzo Barberini, this collection of paintings has works by Raphael, Caravaggio, and Titian, as well as a portrait of Henry VIII by Hans Holbein. Bernini contributed to the overall design of the dramatic building, including the grand staircase at the entrance.

 D2 **19** PALAZZO BARBERINI, VIA DELLE QUATTRO FONTANE 13
06-48-24-184 OR 06-42-00-36-69

MUSEO E GALLERIA BORGHESE
This 17th-century villa holds one of Rome's most choice art collections. Permanent displays include sculptures by Bernini (don't miss the unforgettable marble *Pluto and Proserpina*) and

GALLERIA DELL'ACCADEMIA
DI SAN LUCA

GALLERIA NAZIONALE D'ARTE
ANTICA DI PALAZZO BARBERINI

paintings by Caravaggio, Raphael, and Rubens. Tickets must be purchased in advance.

 PIAZZA SCIPIONE BORGHESE 5
06-32-81-01

PALAZZO MASSIMO ALLE TERME

The museum houses splendid Roman sculptures and antiquities, including an excellent coin collection on the bottom floor. The showstopper is the upstairs room containing frescoes that once graced the walls of Rome's first empress Livia's villa on Monte Palatino (more lavish than that of her husband, Augustus).

 LARGO DI VILLA PERETTI 1
06-48-14-144

SANTA MARIA DELLA CONCEZIONE

The crypt of this church is no ordinary burial place – the bones of some 4,000 capuchin monks, separated into groups of like kind, have been arranged decoratively into patterns on the walls, ceilings, and even as chandeliers.

  VIA VENETO 27
06-48-71-185

TERME DI DIOCLEZIANO

Diocletian's baths, completed in AD 306, were the biggest in ancient Rome, able to accommodate 3,000 bathers at once. Only fragments remain, but it is possible to get a sense of the site's former grandeur by walking around the grounds and visiting the museum.

 VIALE E. DE NICOLA 79
06-39-96-77-00 OR 06-47-82-61-52

MAP 5 COLOSSEO

GALLERIA DORIA PAMPHILJ

The Pamphilj family opens its elegant palace to show off its private collection, including paintings by Caravaggio, Titian, and Guido Reni. Do rent an audio guide here, narrated in excellent

MUSEUM PASSES

Rome's museums are among the world's greatest and oldest. Admission fees have increased considerably in recent years, but you can save quite a bit if you opt for combined ticket options. The most comprehensive is the **Roma Archaeologia Card,** available at the advance reservation window at Colosseo. It costs €20 ($25) and gives you seven days to see the nine included sights: Colosseo, Monte Palatino, Palazzo Massimo, Palazzo Altemps, Crypta Balbi, Terme di Diocleziano, Terme di Caracalla, Villa dei Quintilli, and Mausoleo di Cecelia Metella. (Upstairs exhibits at Colosseo are not included.) **Biglietto unico per il Museo Nazionale Romano** costs €7 ($8.75) is valid for three days for four museums: Palazzo Massimo, Palazzo Altemps, Crypta Balbi, and Terme di Diocleziano. The **Capitolini Card** costs €8.30 ($10.40) is good for seven days at the Musei Capitolini, which includes Palazzo Nuovo, Palazzo dei Conservatori, and the reopened-in-2005 Tabularium e Galleria Lapidaria. It's also good at Centrale Montemartini on Via Ostiense. (Temporary exhibits are not included.)

English by one of the descendants. The classical concerts in this setting are also a treat.

 PIAZZA DEL COLLEGIO ROMANO 2
06-67-97-323

MUSEI CAPITOLINI
See SIGHTS, p. 11.

 PIAZZA DEL CAMPIDOGLIO
06-39-96-78-00 OR 06-67-10-20-71

MUSEO DEL CORSO
Exhibitions at this privately owned museum are smaller in size, but often detail the work and lives of internationally famous artists, writers, and historical figures.

 VIA DEL CORSO 320
06-67-86-209

MUSEO DI PALAZZO VENEZIA
This spectacular palazzo once housed Mussolini's offices, and he made some of his famous speeches from the balcony. Now it's home to a sprawling and varied accumulation of Italian art, including a large collection of porcelain and ceramics and 16th-century frescoes by Giorgio Vasari restored in 2003.

 VIA DEL PLEBESCITO 118
06-67-80-131

MUSEO NAZIONALE D'ARTE ORIENTALE

This old-fashioned museum seems to operate on a shoestring but still has ancient artifacts from the Near East, as well as finds from Tibet and China dating from the 11th to the 18th centuries.

 C5 **28**   VIA MERULANA 248
06-48-74-218

MUSEO PALATINO

Set on the oldest inhabited site in the city, the Antiquarium del Palatino is in a 19th-century villa. Downstairs, artifacts from the hill's Iron Age settlement date back to the 9th century BC, and models of huts show the stomping ground of Romulus. Upstairs, fragments of painting and marble hint at the splendid color of ancient Rome.

 D2 **34**   VIA DI SAN GREGORIO 30
06-39-96-77-00

MUSEO STORICO DELLA LIBERAZIONE DI ROMA

Located on the site where Nazis brought their prisoners for inter-rogation, this museum is a sobering reminder of the atrocities of World War II.

 D6 **41**   VIA TASSO 145
06-70-03-866

SOLIGO ART PROJECT

This modern and contemporary art gallery represents the work of such artists as Valeria Sanguini, Lidia Bachis, and Rita Tagliaferri.

 B3 **14**   VIA CIMARRA 12
06-48-93-02-40

MAP 6 | TRASTEVERE

MUSEO DI ROMA IN TRASTEVERE

A quaint folklore collection in a 17th-century convent for Carmelite nuns, this small museum was renovated in 2000 to include tem-porary gallery space in the cloister, which often hosts exhibits on more contemporary Roman life and festivals.

 B2 **14**   PIAZZA SANT'EGIDIO 1B
06-58-16-563

MAP 7 | VATICANO

ACCADEMIA UNGHERESE

Located in a splendid palace designed in part by Borromini, the Hungarian Academy puts on interesting contemporary art shows that attract a lively international following.

 F6 **41**   PALAZZO FALCONIERI, VIA GIULIA 1
06-68-89-671

GALLERIA NAZIONALE D'ARTE ANTICA
DI PALAZZO CORSINI
A fine example of baroque architecture, this palazzo first greets you with its dramatic stone staircase that leads to noble apartments, where you will find works by Caravaggio, Rubens, Van Dyck, Fra Angelico, and other fine 16th- and 17th-century artists.

 F5🅐38   VIA DELLA LUNGARA 10
06-68-80-23-23

MUSEO STORICO NAZIONALE DELL'ARTE SANITARIA
The medieval medical artifacts at this compelling historical museum will make you appreciate modern medicine. Anatomical charts, which seem primitive today, are displayed along with early surgical tools.

 C4🅐27   LUNGOTEVERE IN SASSIA 3
06-68-93-051

VILLA FARNESINA
Built in the early 16th century as a pleasure villa for a powerful banker, Agostino Chigi, this villa contains beautiful frescoes by Raphael, including a depiction of Galatea pulled by dolphins. Open only in the mornings.

MAP 7 F6🅐40   VIA DELLA LUNGARA 230
06-68-02-72-67 OR 06-68-02-72-68

MUSEI VATICANI (VATICAN MUSEUMS)

GALLERIA DELLE CARTE GEOGRAFICHE

Pope Gregory XIII (of Gregorian calendar fame) designed this 394-foot-long gallery. You can view 16th-century maps of Italy from the observation point at the north end.

MAP 7 B2🅐15   MUSEI VATICANI, VIALE VATICANO
06-69-88-38-60 OR 06-69-88-43-41

MUSEO GREGORIANO EGIZIANO
This museum collects Egyptian art from 2,600 BC–600 BC. Hours vary widely, so call or check at the entrance to be sure that this section is open.

 B2🅐13   MUSEI VATICANI, VIALE VATICANO
06-69-88-38-60 OR 06-69-88-43-41

MUSEO GREGORIANO ETRUSCO
One of the most popular side museums of the Vatican collection, this extensive space contains Greek, Roman, and Etruscan works, including objects from excavations of a well-preserved burial site from 650 BC.

MAP 7 B2🅐14   MUSEI VATICANI, VIALE VATICANO
06-69-88-38-60 OR 06-69-88-43-41

MUSEO GREGORIANO PROFANO
This museum of pagan antiquities includes extensive commentary about the Greek and Roman sculptures displayed.

 B2🅐11   MUSEI VATICANI, VIALE VATICANO
06-69-88-38-60 OR 06-69-88-43-41

VILLA FARNESINA

GALLERIA NAZIONALE
D'ARTE MODERNA

MUSEO PIO-CLEMENTINO

The world's largest collection of classical statues spans 16 rooms at Museo Pio-Clementino. The Laocoön group is one the most important of the antique sculptures due to its direct influence on Renaissance artists at the time it was excavated. Many rare, choice objects are in this collection.

 A2 ●2   MUSEI VATICANI, VIALE VATICANO
06-69-88-38-60 OR 06-69-88-43-41

MUSEO PIO CRISTIANO

Obscure but fascinating early Christian antiquities – including sarcophagi of biblical stories – are found in this Vatican museum.

MAP 7 B2 ●12   MUSEI VATICANI, VIALE VATICANO
06-69-88-38-60 OR 06-69-88-43-41

MUSEO STORICO-ARTISTICO E TESORO

The "Historical-Artistic Museum and Treasury," this small space preserves Vatican artifacts gathered over the centuries, including a marble tabernacle by famed 15th-century Florentine sculptor Donatello.

MAP 7 A2 ●1   MUSEI VATICANI, VIALE VATICANO
06-69-88-38-60 OR 06-69-88-43-41

RAPHAEL ROOMS

This section is filled with frescoes painted by Raphael, including *The School of Athens,* which features likenesses of Plato and Aristotle. Look up at the ceiling painting by his master, Perugino, who had painted these rooms previously – it's the one work that Raphael refused to paint over.

 C2 ●23   MUSEI VATICANI, VIALE VATICANO
06-69-88-38-60 OR 06-69-88-43-41

OVERVIEW MAP AND OFF MAP

CENTRALE MONTEMARTINI

L'Ex Centrale Termoelettrica Giovanni Montemartini was Rome's early electric plant (1911-1913) and is now a converted exhibit space that displays ancient white marble Roman sculptures, bronzes, and mosaics against the backdrop of immense dark machinery.

OVERVIEW MAP **F3** VIA OSTIENSE 106
06-57-48-030

GALLERIA NAZIONALE D'ARTE MODERNA

This gallery has a significant collection of modern Italian art, as well as works by international painters including Cezanne, Klimt, and Kandinsky. Occasional concerts and a lovely outdoor café are among the other attractions.

OVERVIEW MAP **B4** VIALE DELLE BELLE ARTI 131
06-32-29-81

MAXXI

This gargantuan space opened in 2002 on the north side of town and construction will be ongoing until 2008. Exhibits are in various media and genres, and the works are all by 21st-century artists.

OFF MAP VIA GUIDO RENI 6
06-32-10-181 OR 06-32-02-438

MUSEO DELLA VIA OSTIENSE

The exhibit here traces the construction of the Ostian Way, which connected the city with the sea in the 3rd century BC, and shows models of Ostia Antica, the Port of Claudius, and the Port of Trajan as they were in Imperial Rome.

OVERVIEW MAP **E3** PIAZZA DI PORTA SAN PAOLO, VIA R. PERSICHETTI 3
06-57-43-193

MUSEO DELLE MURA DI ROMA

Housed in Porta San Sebastiano, the ancient southern gate into the Eternal City, the Museo delle Mura tells the story of the Aurelian Wall and the construction of Rome's fortress against invaders, begun by Emperor Aurelian in AD 271. There is a small exhibit area, and you can even stand on top of the wall.

OVERVIEW MAP **F5** VIA DI PORTA SAN SEBASTIANO 18
06-70-47-52-84

MUSEO ETRUSCO DI VILLA GIULIA

Villa Giulia – the site of lavish summer parties in the 16th century – holds a fine collection of Etruscan art and artifacts from the Iron Age to the Roman period, primarily found in Lazio. Save time afterward to enjoy its lovely setting in Borghese Park.

OVERVIEW MAP **A3** PIAZZALE DI VILLA GIULIA 9
06-32-26-571

MUSEO NAPOLEONICO

In 1927, the Bonaparte family donated their 16th-century Palazzo Primoli to the city. This bequest included its collection of Napoleonic paintings and artifacts, all set amidst period furnishing – making for a credible experience of the ambience of the times.

OVERVIEW MAP **C3** PIAZZA DI PONTE UMBERTO I
06-68-80-62-86

PERFORMING ARTS

MAP 1 GHETTO/CAMPO DEI FIORI

SALA BALDINI *CONCERTS*
This grand hall on the side of a church has recitals and chamber music concerts almost daily, often at an early hour (5:15 PM) and some evenings.

MAP 1 E6🅐38 PIAZZA CAMPITELLI 9
06-68-71-31-590

TEATRO ARGENTINA *THEATER*
Located near the site of Julius Caesar's assassination in 44 BC, Rome's loveliest major theater was originally the city's opera house but now hosts drama in Italian, sometimes by regional companies. Watch for special performances like an opera staged by Zefferelli, film premiers, or concerts.

MAP 1 C4🅐27 LARGO DI TORRE ARGENTINA 52
06-68-40-00-345

MAP 3 TRIDENTE

CHIESA ANGLICANA DI OGNISSANTI (ALL SAINTS ANGLICAN CHURCH) *CONCERTS*
This wooden church is a charming setting for good concert performances, often by the Orchestra e Coro dell'Accademi d'Opera Italiana, which stages either selections from famous operas or full-scale operas.

MAP 3 B3🅐13 VIA DEL BABUINO 153B
06-78-42-702

METROPOLITAN CINEMA *MOVIE HOUSE*
Although it's a standard multiplex, this cinema next to Piazza del Popolo usually has one film, sometimes two, in English in one of its four theaters.

MAP 3 A3🅐6 VIA DEL CORSO 7
06-32-00-933

TEATRO SISTINA *THEATER*
The 1,500-seat Teatro Sistina primarily features musicals and is a fun night out, even when productions are artistically lightweight

A ROMAN SUMMER

Summer is no longer the wasteland of decades ago, when the city emptied out and few services were available. The Eternal City comes to life outdoors, with performances in courtyards, in city squares, on the banks of the Tiber River, on rooftops, and in archaeological sites. One of the most recent gains was the return of summer opera to **Terme di Caracalla (p. 22).** These events, programmed by **Teatro dell'Opera (p. 73),** had been canceled for years amid controversy about how to use the historic site safely. A visit to **Teatro Romano di Ostia Antica (p. 75)** will let you watch a performance in the same amphitheater enjoyed by patrons 2,000 years ago. You get to see part (although usually not all) of the historic site by night when temperatures are cooler and it is dramatically illuminated. There are also summer film festivals, such as the series hosted on Tiber Island by the Australians. All this performance excitement has even persuaded Romans to stay around and enjoy the summer glory of their city.

or camp. The Roman musical, *Il Rugantino,* is an annual tradition, and local musicians occasionally perform acoustic shows.

 VIA SISTINA 129
06-42-00-711

 VIA VENETO/TERMINI

CHIESA DI SAN PAOLO ENTRO LE MURA *CONCERTS*
This Protestant church – with an English-speaking parish – regularly presents reliable concerts and operas, even if the stage sets are not lavish. There are usually many Anglophones in the audience, too.

 VIA NAPOLI 58
06-48-26-296

GOETHE INSTITUTE *CONCERTS*
Founded in 1988 to promote research in aesthetic, analytic, and scientific aspects of music, Centro Ricerche Musicale offers edgy, modern music in this austere building, a perfect antidote for baroque overload.

 VIA SAVOIA 15
06-85-30-16-66

CHIESA DI SAN
PAOLO ENTRO
LE MURA

SANTA MARIA DEGLI ANGELI

TEATRO DELL'OPERA
DI ROMA

SANTA MARIA DEGLI ANGELI *CONCERTS*
Classical music concerts are held under the magnificent ceiling designed by Michelangelo. The massive open space lends an importance to events, sometimes premiers by local composers.

 D4 27 PIAZZA DELLA REPUBBLICA
06-48-80-812

TEATRO DELL'OPERA DI ROMA *OPERA*
An austere Mussolini facade belies the ornate 19th-century interior at Rome's main opera venue. This house stages world premieres – *Madama Butterfly* debuted here – and classic international works. Ballet and modern dance are occasionally performed, too.

 E3 35 PIAZZA BENIAMINO GIGLI 1
06-48-16-01

WARNER VILLAGE CINEMA MODERNO *MOVIE HOUSE*
This atmospheric movie house is often showing an English-language film on one of its five screens. The U.S.-style lobby offers popcorn and other snacks, and one theater has frescoes, so you have something to look at before the feature starts.

 E3 33 PIAZZA DELLA REPUBBLICA 44/45
06-47-77-91

MAP 5 COLOSSEO

TEATRO ELISEO – TEATRO PICCOLO ELISEO *THEATER*
Don't be put off by the dreary architecture: This theater is one of Rome's most reliable for quality productions. The fare is usually Italian plays or U.S. and European classics in Italian, with the occasional debut.

 B2 9 VIA NAZIONALE 183
06-48-82-114 OR 06-48-87-22-22

TEATRO QUIRINO *THEATER*
Large enough for grand-scale productions, this 986-seat state-owned theater mounts mostly tried-and-true international dramas

performed by Italian actors. The once famously bad acoustics are now better than average.

 A1 2   VIA DELLE VERGINI 7
06-67-94-585, 06-67-90-616, OR 800-01-36-16 (TOLL-FREE)

MAP 6 | TRASTEVERE

NUOVO PASQUINO *MOVIE HOUSE*
Long a favorite with U.S. and British expats, this small, well-worn cinema shows international films exclusively in their original languages – never dubbed – on its three screens.

 B2 12   PIAZZA SANT'EGIDIO 10
06-58-03-622

MAP 7 | VATICANO

ORATORIO DEL GONFALONE *CONCERTS*
This is a wonderfully romantic spot to hear a classical concert surrounded by Mannerist frescoes and trompe l'oeil corkscrew columns. Coro Polifonico Romano runs programs December–May in the beautiful wood choir.

 E5 35   VIA DEL GONFALONE 32A
06-68-75-952

TEATRO DELL'OROLOGIO *THEATER*
Four small spaces (40-99 seats each) spotlight experimental plays – mostly drama – in low-budget, but tightly organized, productions.

 D6 33   VIA DEI FILIPPINI 17A
06-68-30-87-35 OR 06-68-75-550

OVERVIEW MAP AND OFF MAP

AUDITORIUM PARCO DELLA MUSICA *CONCERTS*
Italian architect Renzo Piano designed this striking musical complex located near Olympic Park in northern Rome. With a combined total of more than 7,000 seats, its three concert halls host operas, symphonies, rock concerts, and choirs, and it's also the home of the Accademia Nazionale di Santa Cecilia concert series. A shuttle to this out-of-the-way location operates from Termini station daily 5-11:30 PM.

OFF MAP   VIALE PIETRO DE COUBERTIN 30
06-80-241

FINDING FILMS IN ROME

Sometimes down time in a cinema is just what you need, but the Italian art of dubbing films dramatically reduces the number of films shown in English. The trick to finding an English-language film is to check a daily newspaper and look in the movie listings for "V.O." *(versione originale),* which means that the film will be shown in its original language. Sometimes the title is only given in its Italian name, which is not necessarily a direct translation of the English title; in this case, the names of the actors or director may help guide your choice.

AULA MAGNA DELL'UNIVERSITÀ DI ROMA LA SAPIENZA *CONCERTS*

Most concerts by the Istituzione Universitaria dei Concerti, found-ed after World War II, take place in this fascist-designed space. Music programming varies widely from traditional to experimental and runs October–June.

OVERVIEW MAP C6   PIAZZALE ALDO MORO 5
06-36-10-051 OR 06-36-10-052

TEATRO OLIMPICO *VARIOUS*

Located in the Flaminio neighborhood north of the city center, this large, 1,410-seat theater offers broad programming that can range from traveling productions (sometimes in English) and ballet to flamenco and pop music performances.

OFF MAP   PIAZZA GENTILE DA FABRIANO 17
06-32-65-991

TEATRO ROMANO DI OSTIA ANTICA *THEATER*

This beautifully preserved ancient Roman amphitheater just a short train ride from the city puts on performances of traditional Greek and Roman classics, as well as concerts in the summer. The seats are made of stone, so bring a cushion. Consider coming early to tour the extensive ruins.

OFF MAP   VIALE DEI ROMAGNOLI 717
06-56-35-80-99

TEATRO VITTORIA *THEATER*

This venue has two specialties: theater for children and interna-tional productions, occasionally in English, for adults. The cave-like, 562-seat space makes for great sound.

OVERVIEW MAP E3   PIAZZA SANTA MARIA LIBERATRICE 8
06-57-40-170

RECREATION

 MAP 1 GHETTO/CAMPO DEI FIORI

ROMARENT

Located in the right off Piazza Campo dei Fiori, this bike and moped outfitter offers reasonably priced guided tours of the city, such as an excursion through the ancient ruins outside the city walls.

 MAP 1 B2 **Ⓐ9**   VICOLO DEI BOVARI 7A
06-68-96-555

MAP 3 TRIDENTE

PINCIO

Take the winding street from the eastern corner of Piazza del Popolo and you ascend into the luscious Pincio gardens. Besides being a great place to break up the day's sightseeing with a picnic, it also boasts one of the most spectacular panoramas of the city.

 MAP 3 A3 **Ⓐ4**   TAKE VIALE GABRIELE D'ANNUNZIO FROM PIAZZA DEL POPOLO

VILLA BORGHESE

See SIGHTS, p. 8.

 MAP 3 A6 **✪16**   MAIN ENTRANCE AT PIAZZALE BRASILE

 MAP 4 VIA VENETO/TERMINI

BUS 110

These three-hour bus tours let you hop on and off along the route to explore the sights you're interested in. The accompanying guide has been known to speak several languages. A bus departs from Termini station every 20 minutes, and there are various pick up/ drop off points throughout the city.

MAP 4 E4 **Ⓐ37**   PIAZZA DEI CINQUECENTO, SIDEWALK C (IN FRONT OF TERMINI STATION)
06-46-95-22-52

ENJOY ROME

As the name implies, this unique organization can provide you

ROMARENT   GIANICOLO

with just about anything you may need to enjoy Rome, including reasonably priced walking tours.

  VIA MARGHERA 8A
06-44-51-843

 COLOSSEO

CIRCO MASSIMO
Once a massive ancient Roman stadium used for chariot races and executing criminals, this 650-yard athletic field is now a jogging track. It's a great place to relax and even stages the occasional concert.

  VIALE AVENTINO BTWN. VIA DEL CIRCO MASSIMO AND VIA DEI CERCHI

VILLA CELIMONTANA
Once the property of the powerful Mattei family, this villa on the Celian Hill boasts a public park complete with gardens and swings for the kids. It hosts live jazz concerts in the summer, and the setting couldn't be more perfect.

  PIAZZA DELLA NAVICELLA

MAP 7 VATICANO

GIANICOLO
The Gianicolo (Janiculum Hill) affords Romans the best view of their fair city. On a clear day you can see for miles; at night, the area becomes lovers' lane.

 ENTER AT VIA GARIBALDI AND VIA DEL GIANICOLO

GIARDINI VATICANI
The meticulously manicured Giardini Vaticani (Vatican Gardens) contain statues, lakes, fountains, and of course, numerous flowers.

ALLO STADIO! TO THE STADIUM!

No true experience of Rome is complete without a trip to the Stadio Olimpico (northern Rome, Via Foro Italico, 06-36-851), home of Rome's two rival soccer teams, AS Roma and SS Lazio. The Italian concept of *bella figura* loses all meaning here as screaming fans jump on the seats to cheer for their heroes and taunt the opposing players. Be sure to brace yourself whenever Roma star Francesco Totti scores a goal. Things get especially emotional during the Derby, when the two home teams are pitted against each other. Seat prices for all games range $18–80 (€15–67), and tickets can be bought in advance wherever there is a lotto machine and, for Roma matches, at the AS Roma store (Piazza Colonna 360, 06-67-86-514). Try not to wear any clothing that resembles the colors of the opposing team.

A complete tour of the 40-acre grounds can take several hours and advance reservations are a must.

 C1 ⚫ 21 CENTRO SERVIZI, PIAZZA DI SAN PIETRO
06-69-88-44-66

ORTO BOTANICO (BOTANICAL GARDEN)
This lush expanse behind Palazzo Corsini includes thousands of plant species and a fascinating garden of scents and tactile sensations for the blind.

 F5 ⚫ 39 LARGO CRISTINA DI SVEZIA 24
06-68-64-193

OVERVIEW MAP

VILLA ADA
A popular park among local runners and picnickers, the Villa Ada is just north of the city center and has refreshingly peaceful ponds and lakes.

OVERVIEW MAP **A5** ENTER AT VIA SALARIA AND VIA DI VILLA ADA

VILLA DORIA PAMPHILI
A glimpse of the massive ancient Roman aqueduct that surrounds it is more than enough to justify a visit. There are also numerous jogging trails, as well as picnic spots and play areas for kids.

OVERVIEW MAP **D1** ENTER AT VIA DI SAN PANCRAZIO AND LARGO 3
GIUGNO 1849

H HOTELS

Most old-world charm: **HASSLER VILLA MEDICI**, p. 82

Friendliest owner: **RESIDENZA ZANARDELLI**, p. 80

Best art nouveau decor: **LOCARNO**, p. 83

Celebrity favorite: **HOTEL DE RUSSIE**, p. 82

Best spa: **HOTEL EXEDRA**, p. 84

Grandest lobby for a rendezvous: **REGINA BAGLIONI**, p. 85

PRICE KEY

$ ROOMS UNDER US$200

$$ ROOMS US$200-300

$$$ ROOMS OVER US$300

MAP 1 GHETTO/CAMPO DEI FIORI

ALBERGO DEL SOLE AL BISCIONE *QUAINT* $

Built near the ruins of the Teatro di Pompeo, this 58-room updated pension has the atmosphere of a cozy inn. Some rooms have a vista of Campo dei Fiori.

MAP 1 B2 **11** VIA DEL BISCIONE 76
06-68-80-68-73

HOTEL TIZIANO *CHIC* $$

The best choice for upscale lodging near Campo dei Fiori, the Tiziano is both luxurious (Egyptian cotton linens) and practical (English-speaking staff).

MAP 1 B3 **13** CORSO VITTORIO EMANUELE II 110
06-68-65-019

TEATRO DI POMPEO *QUAINT* $

Ancient architecture and friendly hospitality come together at Teatro di Pompeo, built near the site of Julius Caesar's assassination. Guest rooms have wood ceiling beams from the 15th century.

MAP 1 C2 **23** LARGO DEL PALLARO 8
06-68-72-812

MAP 2 PIAZZA NAVONA/PANTHEON

CESARI *QUAINT* $$

In the mid-19th century, Stendhal was a frequent guest at this small, quiet hotel. Today, the renovated interior has contemporary muted hues and marble bathrooms.

MAP 2 B6 **36** VIA DI PIETRA 89A
06-67-49-701

HOTEL RAPHAËL *ROMANTIC* $$$

With guest rooms fashioned by Florentine designers and a lobby decorated with Picasso ceramics, this ivy-covered hideaway touts its service and attention to detail. The classical surroundings are balanced with such modern amenities as a gym.

MAP 2 B2 **20** LARGO FEBO 2
06-68-28-31

RESIDENZA ZANARDELLI *ROMANTIC* $

Silk wallpaper by Versace and other elegant details add to the charm of this seven-room residence. The gregarious Australian-Italian owners create an intimate atmosphere that is both familial and private.

MAP 2 A2 **3** VIA ZANARDELLI 7
06-68-21-13-92

SANTA CHIARA *QUAINT* $$

The same family has owned and operated this bastion of hospitali-

HOTEL TIZIANO   HOTEL RAPHAËL   DEI BORGOGNONI

ty since the mid-1800s. Small rooms offer marble desks and baths, and several overlook a lovely piazza.

 MAP 2 C4 🄷44 VIA SANTA CHIARA 21
06-68-72-979

SOLE AL PANTHEON *QUAINT* *$$$*
This hotel claims the Pantheon as its next-door neighbor – a location that's hard to resist. The rooms are small, but high ceilings and tile floors add to the illusion of space.

MAP 2 B4 🄷32 PIAZZA DELLA ROTONDA 63
06-67-80-441

MAP 3 TRIDENTE

CASA HOWARD *CHIC* *$$*
Popular with people in the film industry, Casa Howard is a playground for the jet set. All the furnishings are one-of-a-kind designs, and the Chinese Room, with its Turkish bath, is exquisite.

 MAP 3 E5 🄷61 VIA CAPO LE CASE 18
06-69-92-45-55

DEI BORGOGNONI *CHIC* *$$$*
Amazingly quiet despite its location in Rome's shopping corridor, this small hotel is within walking distance of most major sights in the city. Rooms are comfortable and elegant.

 MAP 3 E5 🄷62 VIA DEL BUFALO 126
06-69-94-15-05

DE LA VILLE INTER-CONTINENTAL *GRAND* *$$$*
The grand lobby gives no hint that the rooms are austere, but its prime location at the top of the Spanish Steps draws business and international travelers.

 MAP 3 D5 🄷45 VIA SISTINA 69
06-67-331

GREGORIANA HOTEL *QUAINT* *$*
The Gregoriana is a good value in the Tridente neighborhood. Its small rooms are soundproof and spare, but accents like lush red

SEASIDE SPLURGE

Live like J. Paul Getty for a night or two at **La Vecchia Posta** (Palo Laziale, Ladispoli, 06-99-49-501; $$$), Getty's former villa on the sea and one of Rome's most decadent getaway hotels. Located just 10 minutes north of Rome's Fiumincino Airport near Ladispoli, the hotel has a beautiful setting on the coast, where the Mediterranean to the west laps against the seawall and produces a magnificent sunset every day. Indoors, the scenery is also wonderful, as the curator of Getty's museum acquired the furniture and art. In addition, the excellent service and garden-grown meals will make you feel like an invited guest. The building itself was once the Odescalchi family's guesthouse – they're the ones with the castle next door – and, before Getty purchased it, last served as a post office inn. The villa was restored in the 1960s, and ancient ruins and artifacts discovered during the renovations are now displayed in a private underground museum. All this luxury comes with a hefty price tag, but if you can swing it, the experience is unique.

fabrics keep them from being austere. There's no restaurant, but an attentive staff delivers breakfast every morning.

 VIA GREGORIANA 18
06-67-97-988

HASSLER VILLA MEDICI   *ROMANTIC* $$$
Offering stunning views of Rome, this famous hotel draws Hollywood stars and world leaders who seek its discretion and excellent service. The classically decorated rooms are elegant and reserved.

 PIAZZA DELLA TRINITÀ DEI MONTI 6
06-69-93-40

HOTEL DE RUSSIE   *CHIC* $$$
Frequented by many in the entertainment industry, this hotel, with its neutral tones and modern decor, offers an alternative to the antiquity of Rome. It boasts a spa and good dining, as well as a lobby bar that's a destination for locals and travelers alike.

 VIA DEL BABUINO 9
06-32-88-81

HOTEL D'INGHILTERRA   *ROMANTIC* $$
Once the home of Torlonia princes, this property, with its small but luxurious rooms, now hosts weary shoppers. The hotel's art collection enhances the stately decor.

 VIA BOCCA DI LEONE 14
06-69-981

HOTEL DE RUSSIE   HASSLER VILLA MEDICI   LOCARNO

HOTEL DUE TORRE   *QUAINT*   *$$*

This reasonably priced hotel with small, comfortable rooms is centrally located near Piazza Navona but has the benefit of being tucked away from the bustle.

MAP 3 E1 ⑪51   VICOLO DEL LEONETTO 23
06-68-80-69-56

HOTEL PORTOGHESI   *QUAINT*   *$*

This tiny hotel has a roof garden with exquisite vistas. Its small rooms are generously furnished with copies of antiques, and the service is friendly and discreet.

MAP 3 F1 ⑪65   VIA DEI PORTOGHESI 1
06-68-64-231

HOTEL VALADIER   *ROMANTIC*   *$$$*

Located between the Spanish Steps and Piazza del Popolo, Valadier offers opulent rooms, marble baths, a roof terrace with panoramic views, and professional service.

MAP 3 B3 ⑪10   VIA DELLA FONTANELLA 15
06-36-11-998

LOCARNO   *CHIC*   *$$*

The Locarno's art nouveau doors lead to two distinct and inviting wings: an older, traditional section and a contemporary, all-suites addition. The rooftop is open for drinks, too.

MAP 3 A2 ⑪3   VIA DELLA PENNA 22
06-36-10-841

PLAZA   *GRAND*   *$$$*

Built in 1860, the Plaza has retained a fin de siècle ambience. Rooms are furnished with original antiques, but guests can expect 21st-century amenities.

MAP 3 D3 ⑪31   VIA DEL CORSO 126
06-69-92-11-11

SCALINATA DI SPAGNA   *QUAINT*   *$$*

A good value near pricey Piazza di Spagna, this small, 16-room hotel is easy to miss even though it's right at the top of the steps. Be sure to book months in advance.

MAP 3 D5 ⑪44   PIAZZA DELLA TRINITÀ DEI MONTI 17
06-67-93-006

MAP 4 VIA VENETO/TERMINI

BAILEY'S *CHIC $$*

Bailey's delivers modern elegance and such amenities as fast Internet connections and eager-to-please service in its marble surroundings.

 C3 **14** VIA FLAVIA 39
06-42-02-04-86

BERNINI BRISTOL *QUAINT $$*

A Roman favorite since 1870, the genteel Bristol offers opulent rooms that are elegant rather than gaudy. The Piazza Barberini location is handy for shoppers and transportation.

 D2 **18** PIAZZA BARBERINI 23
06-48-83-051

EMPIRE PALACE HOTEL *GRAND $$*

The spacious rooms feature original contemporary paintings and tasteful antiques. The hotel bar brings in a local crowd every night.

 C3 **13** VIA AURELIANA 39
06-42-12-81

EXCELSIOR *GRAND $$$*

Once one of the most lavish hotels, the Excelsior still attracts heads of state and wealthy tycoons, who can't resist its Via Veneto location. However, the lobby, with its worn upholstery, is showing its age.

 C2 **9** VIA VENETO 125
06-47-081

HOTEL EDEN *GRAND $$$*

Reputed to be Fellini's favorite hotel in Rome, the Eden stands in an area once known for la dolce vita. The rooms are understated and conservative, while La Terrazza restaurant gives diners a rooftop view of Rome.

 C1 **5** VIA LUDOVISI 49
06-47-81-21

HOTEL EXEDRA *GRAND $$$*

Since it opened in 2002, the Exedra has transformed Piazza della Repubblica into a classier address. One wing was converted from an ex-monastery and offers small but cozy rooms with historic details. The tranquil spa will pamper you with personal attention.

 E3 **32** PIAZZA DELLA REPUBBLICA 47
06-48-93-81

MAJESTIC *GRAND $$$*

This grand hotel offers good service without pretension. The period antiques gives it a 19th-century air, but stop in at the bar for a surprising soundtrack of '70s pop music.

 C1 **6** VIA VENETO 50
06-42-14-41

EXCELSIOR   ST. REGIS GRAND

REGINA BAGLIONI *GRAND* *$$$*

The sumptuous lobby greets you with oriental rugs, silk wall coverings, and original antiques; the exceptionally large rooms continue the extravagance with plush furnishings.

 C2 **H11** VIA VENETO 72
06-42-11-11

RESIDENZA CELLINI *CHIC* *$$*

The former home of a countess, Residenza Cellini offers six exceptionally large, light-filled rooms. Beds have orthopedic mattresses, and some bathrooms have hot tubs.

 D3 **H23** VIA MODENA 5
06-47-82-52-04

ST. REGIS GRAND *GRAND* *$$$*

Every room at the St. Regis has a hand-painted fresco above the bed. Murano glass chandeliers grace the lobby, and the fine service matches the elegant environment.

 D3 **H21** VIA VITTORIO EMANUELE ORLANDO 3
06-47-091

MAP 5 COLOSSEO

DOMUS AVENTINA *QUAINT* *$*

A very Roman hotel, even down to the classical artifacts in the lobby, this small, gracious establishment has well-appointed rooms, and its location makes it a good base for exploring the city's major archaeological sites.

 F1 **H46** VIA DI SANTA PRISCA 11B
06-57-46-135

DUCA D'ALBA *ROMANTIC* *$*

This hotel's neoclassical decor is stylish and elegant: Soundproof rooms have custom-made furnishings, and bathrooms gleam with Carrara marble.

 B3 **H17** VIA LEONINA 12
06-48-44-71

HOTEL CELIO *ROMANTIC* $

More of an inn than a hotel, the Celio is visually stunning with original murals and custom furniture. Located right behind the Colosseum, it's convenient for touring the Roman Forum.

 D4 **39** VIA DEI SANTI QUATTRO 35C
06-70-49-53-33

TREVI *ROMANTIC* $

Located on a side street near its namesake fountain, this little and little-known hotel offers tranquility and privacy in an otherwise bustling area.

 A1 **3** VICOLO DEL BABUCCIO 20
06-67-89-563

MAP 6 | TRASTEVERE

RIPA HOTEL *CHIC* $$

The Ripa's seedy side-street location and postindustrial facade give a dubious first impression. But inside, there's an eminently professional staff to greet you and a modern, minimalist decor that features recessed lighting and ergonomic chairs.

 E2 **27** VIA DEGLI ORTI DI TRASTEVERE 3
06-58-611

VILLA SAN PIO *QUAINT* $$

The decor here is ornate Venetian, in contrast to the nearby archaeological sites. Enjoy the manicured gardens, and discover the hidden grape arbors on the grounds.

 F6 **30** VIA SANTA MELANIA 19
06-57-83-214

MAP 7 | VATICANO

ATLANTE STAR *GRAND* $$

The grandest hotel near St. Peter's, the Atlante Star draws even non-guests to its 5,000-square-foot roof garden with its panorama of the city. Antique-filled rooms each have a marble bathroom with hot tub.

 B4 **18** VIA VITELLESCHI 34
06-68-73-233

BRAMANTE *ROMANTIC* $

The perfect base for a Vatican-centered visit, the Bramante offers privacy and personalized service in its elegant but spare, high-ceilinged rooms.

 C4 **25** VICOLO DELLE PALLINE 24-25
06-68-80-64-26

RIPA HOTEL   ATLANTE STAR   CAVALIERI HILTON

OVERVIEW MAP AND OFF MAP

CAVALIERI HILTON   *GRAND* *$$$*
Perched on one of Rome's outlying hills, the Hilton presents old
world formality alongside modern comforts like 24-hour room
service. The on-site restaurant, Heinz Beck's La Pergola, is reason
enough to stay here. You may be three miles away from the city
center, but the balcony views, lush surroundings, and plentiful
diversions (like wine tastings and a gorgeous pool) make it a destination in itself.

OFF MAP   VIA ALBERTO CADLOLO 101
              06-35-091

LORD BYRON   *CHIC* *$$$*
One of the city's few art deco hotels, this town house borders
Villa Borghese. The discreet service suits the demanding, stylish
clientele.

OVERVIEW MAP A3   VIA G. DE NOTARIS 5
                      06-32-20-404

PARCO DEI PRINCIPI   *CHIC* *$$$*
North of Rome's historic center, Parco dei Principi provides spacious rooms and a lovely swimming pool, a rarity in this densely
packed city. Deluxe rooms come with views of Villa Borghese and
St. Peter's.

OVERVIEW MAP A4   VIA G. FRESCOBALDI 5
                      06-85-44-21

CITY ESSENTIALS

LEONARDO DA VINCI AIRPORT (FIUMICINO)

Most international and domestic flights into Rome land at Fiumicino (06-65-951, www.adr.it), located approximately 20 miles southwest of the city center on the coast. The most cost-efficient way to get into the city is via a special nonstop train called the Leonardo Express, which goes directly to the Termini Central Train Station every 20 minutes. After you collect your luggage, simply follow the signs to the Stazione Ferroviaria (railway station), and purchase the ticket either at the window right before the tracks, or from one of the several automated machines on the platforms. The ride costs about $12 each way and takes approximately 30 minutes. Don't forget to validate the ticket in one of the small yellow machines located along the platform. A taxi ride into the city center takes 40-60 minutes, depending on traffic, and will cost $50-70.

Most of the low cost airlines, such as Ryan Air and EasyJet land at Ciampino Fiumicino (06-65-951, www.adr.it), a small part-military, part-civilian airport located about 12 miles east of the city center. A Terravision shuttle bus (06-79-49-45-72, www.terravision.it) leaves for Termini Central Train Station every 30 minutes. Tickets cost about $10 each way and can be purchased on the flight or at the Terravision ticket window after passport control. The trip takes 30-40 minutes, depending on traffic.

ARRIVING OR DEPARTING BY TRAIN

Although there are plans to change the name of Rome's central train station to Stazione Giovanni Paolo II after the late pope, for now it still called Termini (06-47-84-11, www.roma-termini.it or www.grandestazione.it) and is located on the east side of the city center near Piazza dei Cinquecento. Many city buses and both subway lines stop at Termini station.

The state-run agency Trenitalia (89-20-21, www.trenitalia.it) handles most of the train service in the country. There is an extensive website where you can check schedules and fare information and buy tickets (only with a reservation). Be aware of frequent strikes and other disruptions, which can result in extremely limited service. Numerous automatic kiosks around Termini station are the best way to purchase tickets and get schedule or fare information as the lines at the *biglietteria* (ticket window) are often slow and long. The Eurostar, a high-speed train with frequent service to all of the major cities in Italy, departs Termini station for Florence (Firenze Santa Maria Novella, $36 one way) and Milan (Milano Centrale, $50 one way) approximately every hour except for late evenings and during the night.

Rome's smaller train station, Stazione Tiburtina, is located on the east side of the city. The Metro B line and several buses in

the adjoining piazza (Piazzale della Stazione Tiburtina) provide frequent service to the city center. Coach buses offering
departures to several smaller Italian cities leave from the bus
terminal on the opposite end of the station.

PUBLIC TRANSPORTATION

The Rome public transportation company, ATAC (80-04-31-
784, www.atac.roma.it), runs an extensive network of buses
and trams throughout the city and its environs. There are also
two metro (subway) lines, the A (red) and the B (blue), and the
same tickets are utilized for the metro, tram, and bus (about
$1.25). Tickets must be purchased in advance at *tabacchi* or
newsstands bearing the ATAC logo. Remember that tickets must
be validated in the small yellow machines located in the front
and back of the bus, while metro tickets are validated at turn-
stiles in the station. Tickets are good for unlimited tram and bus
transfers during a 75-minute period and for one transfer on the
metro. Weeklong passes are available for less than $15. You can
pick up bus and subway maps at newsstands, subway stations,
and tourist information centers throughout the city.

The subway stops running at 11:30 PM on weekdays and 12:30
AM on weekends, but service tends to be sporadic after 10 PM.
Due to renovations that are scheduled to be completed in
late 2006, the Metro A line stops running at 9 PM, at which
point it is replaced by a bus that stops at all of the stations
along the route.

Most buses run seven days a week until midnight unless otherwise indicated. Night buses are indicated by an owl logo on
the signposts at major stops and run approximately every 30
minutes 12:30 AM–5 AM.

TAXIS

All licensed taxis have meters (refuse a ride if there isn't one),
and rates start at about $3, increasing incrementally accord-
ing to time and distance. There's an extra charge of €1 (about
$1.25) for each piece of luggage placed in the trunk. Tipping
usually involves simply rounding up to the next euro. There
are taxi stands in major tourist areas, and you can call for
one as well. Flagging one down is possible but is not the most
effective way of getting a ride.

RADIO TAXI 06-35-70 OR 06-66-45

COOPERATIVA SAMARCANDA 06-55-51

DRIVING AND RENTING A CAR

U.S. driver's licenses are valid in Italy. Driving in Rome is a
difficult proposition, as lanes tend not to be honored, and
mopeds, which seem to be everywhere, make their own
rules. Parking, too, is difficult. Public garages are not only

expensive, but there are very few of them in the city center. Some neighborhoods have metered parking indicated by blue lines painted on the street, while others are restricted from car traffic altogether. The ZTL (limited traffic zone) varies in each neighborhood around the center. Keep an eye out for signs and video cameras, as straying into the ZTL without a permit can result in a fine (if you're in a rental, the agency will charge your credit card for the amount of the fine).

Rental car prices vary widely, ranging $18–40 per day, not including hefty taxes and additional insurance charges that run upwards of 20 percent. Rates also depend on the day of the week and the season. The major international rental companies are all represented in Rome, as are many locally owned companies. Many are closed on Sundays, except at the airport and Termini station, so make sure your branch is open when you plan to pick up and return your vehicle.

AVIS 06-65-01-15-31 (FIUMICINO), 06-48-14-373 (TERMINI), 19-91-00-133 (INFORMATION/RESERVATIONS)

HERTZ 06-65-01-15-53 (FIUMICINO), 06-47-40-389 (TERMINI), 19-91-12-211 (INFORMATION/RESERVATIONS)

SIXT 06-65-95-35-478 (FIUMICINO), 19-91-00-666 (INFORMATION/RESERVATIONS)

VISITOR INFORMATION

The Rome Tourism Board operates several kiosks throughout the city. They are generally open 9:30 AM–7:30 PM and can provide you with city and public transport maps, hotel reservations, general information, and itineraries. There are kiosks located near every major sight and attraction, including Fiumicino Airport (Terminal B), Piazza delle Cinque Lune (near Piazza Navona), Piazza dei Cinquecento (right outside Termini Station), Piazza Pia (near Castel Sant'Angelo), and Piazza Sidney Sonnino (in Trastevere).

ROME TOURISM BOARD (MAIN OFFICE)
 VIA PARIGI 5
06-48-89-91 (BROCHURES) OR 06-82-05-91-27 (QUESTIONS)
WWW.ROMATURISMO.IT

CURRENCY EXCHANGE

Most banks in Rome are open Mon.–Fri. 8:30 AM–4:30 PM, though they tend to close for an hour at lunch, starting at 1:30 PM. ATM cards issued by U.S. banks can be used to withdraw cash from Italian ATMs (Bancomat). Commissions on currency exchange vary; some charge a percentage, while others charge a flat fee. All banks other than commercial ones will exchange foreign currency, and most will cash travelers checks and give cash advances to Visa cardholders. There are several exchange bureaus around the city center that all have more or less the same rate.

AMERICAN EXPRESS
 D5 PIAZZA DI SPAGNA 38
06-67-641

TRAVELEX ITALIA
 D2 PIAZZA BARBERINI 21A
06-42-02-01-50

EMBASSIES

BRITISH EMBASSY
MAP 4 B4 VIA XX SETTEMBRE 80
06-42-20-00-01
WWW.BRITAIN.IT

CANADIAN EMBASSY
OVERVIEW MAP B5 VIA ZARA 30
06-44-59-81

U.S. EMBASSY
MAP 4 C2 VIA VENETO 119A
06-46-741
WWW.USEMBASSY.IT

WEATHER

Rome is hot and humid in summer, when temperatures can
reach well into the 90s. Spring and fall are mild, and most
of the city's rainfall occurs in March, April, September, and
November. Winters are also mild, with average temperatures
staying in the 50s, though many public spaces are not heated.

HOURS

Rome is not a particularly late-night city, especially where dining is concerned. Restaurants usually close around 1 AM and
usually don't have reservations after 11 PM. Neighborhoods
with the greatest concentration of after-hours bars and cafés
include Trastevere and the Piazza Navona/Pantheon area. In
general, shops are open Mon.-Fri. 10 AM-1 PM and 4-7 PM, though
in tourist areas, many stay open all day. Most tourist sights
have different hours depending on the season and stop letting
in visitors one hour prior to closure. Parks are generally open
from dawn until dusk. The majority of businesses close for all
or part of August when most Italians head to the seaside.

FESTIVALS AND EVENTS

There always seems to be some type of festivity going on in
Rome, especially during the summer months. Many smaller
festivals almost seem spur of the moment, with market stands
and impromptu parades suddenly appearing in the piazzas and
streets. Pick up a copy of *Roma C'è*, magazine at any news-
stand to find out what's going on.

MARCH/APRIL

Roma Independent Film Festival: Various theaters around
the city screen both Italian and international independent films, which are often subtitled in English. Late March.
(Various locations, 06-45-42-50-50, www.riff.it)

Settimana Santa (Holy Week): Every neighborhood church in Rome hosts religious processions and street fairs during the week leading up to Easter, with the Borgo quarter near the Vatican being especially lively. The festivities close with the *via Crucis*, the procession which emulates Jesus's walk to the cross, and of course, a papal blessing. Week leading up to Easter. (Various locations)

Festival Internazionale di Fotografia (Rome International Photography Festival): This series of photo exhibitions throughout the city is meant to promote social awareness. Mid-April–mid-June. (Various locations, 06-49-27-141, www. fotografiafestival.it)

MAY/JUNE

Estate Romana (Roman Summer): This extravaganza of major events around the city includes fashion, film, theater, music, and dance productions. May–September. (Various locations, www.estateromana2002.it)

Festival Internazionale delle Letterature (International Literature Festival): Local actors read works of international writers and poets in Italian every evening 9 PM–1 AM. Late May–late June. (Basilica di Massenzio in the Foro Romano, 06-82-07-73-04, www.festivaldelleletterature.it)

Notti Animate a Castel Sant'Angelo (Animated Evenings at Castel Sant'Angelo): This ancient castle opens its doors in the evenings to host plays, mimes, and musicians in a historic setting. Mid-June–July. (Castel Sant'Angelo, 06-32-86-91, www.castelsantangelo.com)

Notti di Cinema a Piazza Vittorio (Cinema Nights at Piazza Vittorio): This piazza in the heart of Rome's immigrant quarter hosts several international film series throughout the summer. There are also several culturally themed stands offering artisan goods and food at great prices. June–September. (Piazza Vittorio, 06-44-51-208)

Villa Celimontana Jazz: Most jazz venues in the city sponsor outdoor summer concerts in this huge park. June–September. (Villa Celimontana, 06-58-97-807, www. villacelimontanajazz.com)

Festa della Unita (Unity Festival): The Democrats of the Left, a major Italian political party, sponsors this huge yearly event of concerts, cuisine, and games that takes place in a former industrial complex on the south side of the city. Late June–late July. (Mercati Generali on Via Ostiense, www.festaunita.it)

JULY

I Concerti Nel Parco (Concerts in the Park): These concerts range from classical to rock (previous participants include Patti Smith and Ennio Morricone), and most boast such accompaniments as theater, magic shows, and wine tasting. July. (Villa Pamphilj, 06-58-16-987, www.iconcertinelparco.it)

OCTOBER/NOVEMBER

RomaEuropa Festival: This annual modern arts celebration puts on nightly dance, cinema, theater, and music performances. October–November, (Various locations, www.romaeuropa.net)

Roma Jazz Festival: This internationally renowned event is dedicated entirely to jazz and its composers. Late October–late November. (Auditorium Parco della Musica, 06-56-30-50-15, www.romajazzfestival.it)

DECEMBER

Festival Romics (Comics and Animation Festival): Italy's most popular comic artists and animators come together to share ideas and critique each other's work at this annual gathering. Early December. (Fiera di Roma, 06-93-95-51-08, www.romics.it)

Natale e Santo Stefano (Christmas and St. Stefano): Christmas is marked by a plethora of masses and processions around the Vatican. A trip to the nativity scene in St. Peter's Square is not to be missed. December 25. (Vaticano)

DISABLED ACCESS

Rome is not a terribly accessible city as far as wheelchair ramps and sight access go. There are buses that accommodate wheelchair users, but it's important to call ATAC (06-46-95-40-01) ahead of time to check current availability and routes.

SAFETY

Crime in Rome tends toward theft rather than more violent acts. Pickpockets are prevalent on crowded buses and the metro, and cars are often targets as well (always remove valuables). Be wary of bands of beggars with children in tow. A common scheme is for the "mother" to distract you by pulling on your clothing and asking for change while the children pilfer your belongings. The metro is particularly notorious for pickpockets, so be very cautious. As in any big city, use caution when traveling in unfamiliar areas, especially at night. The area immediately around Termini station is especially unsavory, where unsuspecting tourists are known to be preyed upon.

HEALTH AND EMERGENCY SERVICES

The general emergency number (free from any phone) is 113. If you need an ambulance, dial 118. The direct line for the fire department is 115. The police department also maintains a hot line in English at 112. The Aventino Medical Group is a medical practice primarily run by U.S.-trained physicians. Don't leave home without ascertaining that your health insurance policy will cover you in Italy. Citizens of the EU are automatically covered, but U.S. residents must provide their own coverage.

AVENTINO MEDICAL GROUP

MAP 5 F2 VIA DELLA FONTE DI FAUNO 22
06-57-80-738 WWW.AVENTINOMEDICALGROUP.COM

ROME AMERICAN HOSPITAL
OFF MAP VIA E. LONGONI 69
06-22-551 WWW.RAH.IT

PHARMACIES

Pharmacies are indicated by an illuminated green cross and there are several located throughout the city. Every pharmacy is required to post the nearest location that is open 24 hours or is at least on call for emergencies. This location rotates every week. Pharmacists are well versed in prescription medications and can legally offer advice and help. They also routinely prescribe herbal and homeopathic remedies to treat minor ailments.

FARMACIA INTERNAZIONALE BARBERINI

MAP 4 D1 PIAZZA BARBERINI 49
06-48-25-456

FARMACIA TRINITÀ DEI MONTI

MAP 3 D5 PIAZZA DI SPAGNA 30
06-67-90-626

PIRAM

MAP 4 E3 VIA NAZIONALE 228
06-48-80-754

MEDIA AND COMMUNICATIONS

All the phone numbers in this book are listed as they would be dialed within Rome. Rome telephone numbers do not have a set number of digits, but rather vary between five and eight. Most numbers begin with 06 and cell phone numbers begin with a 3. Service phone numbers usually begin with an 8. Dial 12 for Italian directory assistance and 170 for an international operator.

You must buy a *scheda telefonica* if you need to use a pay phone. These are telephone cards with preset spending limits and are available at *tabacchi* and newsstands in denominations as low as €2.50. Tear off the corner of the card where indicated before inserting it into the slot. International calls can be made with calling cards from pay phones without a card, provided you have a toll-free access number. There are very few coin-operated public phones, but phone centers, which offer rates as low as €0.10 per minute, are scattered throughout the city.

The Italian postal service has branches throughout Rome, identified by yellow signs with a "PT" logo. Normal hours are Mon.-Fri., 8:30 AM-5:30 PM, although most close an hour for lunch, usually around 1:30 PM. Some are open Saturday mornings as well. Letter rates within Italy begin at €0.45, while an international letter runs €0.80. Most *tabacchi* offer postage stamps so you can avoid the long wait at the post office.

Italy's two main newspapers are *Corriere della Sera* and *La Repubblica*. The English-language *International Herald Tribune* (owned by the *New York Times*) is available at most newsstands in the city center. The English-language publication, *Wanted in Rome* (www.wantedinrome.com), comes out twice per month and contains extensive information on cultural events as well as restaurant/nightlife listings.

INTERNET

Most hotels offer Internet access in public areas for a nominal fee, though beware of hidden in-room charges. Some moped/bike rental shops, money wiring outlets, and bars around the center have a few computers with Internet service available for about $3.50 an hour. You can also stop in at an Internet café.

EASY INTERNET BARBERINI
MAP 4 D2 · VIA BARBERINI 2
06-42-90-33-88
WWW.EASYINTERNETCAFE.COM

EASY INTERNET TRASTEVERE
MAP 6 B5 · PIAZZA IN PISCINULA 15
06-58-99-491
WWW.EASYINTERNETCAFE.COM

KOKONET
MAP 7 C4 · VICOLO D'ORFEO 13
06-68-77-264
WWW.KOKONET.ORG

SMOKING

Rome was once a smoker's paradise, but in January 2005, the Italian Parliament passed one of the strictest antismoking laws in Europe. Smoking is now banned in all restaurants, bars, cafés, and public offices.

TIPPING

Most dining establishments include a small service charge in the bill, usually listed as *pane e coperto* (bread and cover) but it is customary to round up to the next euro, or even to add 5 percent more if service is exceptional.

DRY CLEANERS

There's a dry cleaner on almost every corner in the city. If you can't find one, simply ask for a *tintoria* or *lavanderia*. Most hotels offer one-day service at slightly higher rates.

BOLLE BLU
MAP 4 C5 · VIA MONTEBELLO 11
06-45-43-82-37

ROSSELLA CASTAGNA
MAP 1 B5 · VIA DEL GESÙ 66
06-69-94-25-24

ITALIAN PHRASES

Known as the language of poetry and love, Italian is perhaps the most musical language in the world. Speaking it is both fun and theatrical (moving your hands becomes natural) and not very difficult, since in most cases, words are pronounced exactly as they are written. With so many tourists passing through their city, Romans are accustomed to hearing foreign tongues and accents and have an open and playful attitude about helping you speak their language. They are also eager to show off their ability to speak English. So relax and get used to saying the most common expression, *"va bene"* (it's going fine).

THE BASICS

ENGLISH	ITALIAN	PRONUNCIATION
Good day	**Buon giorno**	*bwon jor-no*
Good evening	**Buona sera**	*bwo-na say-ra*
Welcome	**Benvenuto**	*ben-ven-oo-to*
Excuse me	**Mi scusi**	*mee skoo-zee*
Pardon	**Permesso**	*per-mes-so*
Sir	**Signore**	*seen-yor-ay*
Madam	**Signora**	*seen-yor-ah*
Miss	**Signorina**	*seen-yor-ee-na*
Do you speak English?	**Parla inglese?**	*par-la een-glay-zay*
I don't speak Italian	**Non parlo italiano**	*non par-lo ee-tal-ya-no*
How are you? (formal)	**Come sta?**	*ko-may sta*
Very well, thank you	**Molto bene, grazie**	*mole-tow be-nay grat-see-ay*
How's it going? (informal)	**Come va?**	*ko-may va*
It's going fine	**Va bene**	*va be-nay*
My name is...	**Mi chiamo...**	*mee kee-a-mo*
What's your name?	**Come si chiama?**	*ko-may see kee-a-ma*
Please	**Per favore**	*payr fa-vor-ray*
Thank you	**Grazie**	*grat-see-ay*
You're welcome	**Prego**	*pray-go*
I'm sorry	**Mi dispiace**	*mee dees-pee-ah-chay*
Goodbye	**Arrivederci; ciao**	*ar-ree-ve-der-chee; chow*
Yes	**Sì**	*see*
No	**No**	*no*

GETTING AROUND

How do I get to...?	**Come posso andare a...**	*ko-may pohs-so an-da-ray a...*
Where is...?	**Dove**	*do-vay*
the subway	**la metro**	*la met-ro*
the airport	**l'aeroporto**	*lay-ro-por-to*

the train station	**la stazione di treno**	*la stats-yo-nay dee tray-no*
the train	**il treno**	*eel tray-no*
the bus stop	**la fermata dell'autobus**	*la fair-ma-tah day-la-ow-to-boos*
the bus	**l'autobus**	*la ow-to-boos*
the exit	**l'uscita**	*le oo-shee-ta*
the street	**la strada**	*la stra-da*
the garden	**il giardino**	*eel jar-dee-no*
the tourist office	**l'ufficio turistico**	*loof-fee-cho too-rees-tee-ko*
a taxicab	**un taxi**	*oon tak-see*
a hotel	**un albergo**	*oon al-bair-go*
a toilet	**la toilette**	*la twa-let*
a pharmacy	**una farmacia**	*oo-na farm-a-chee-a*
a bank	**una banca**	*oo-na bang-ka*
a telephone	**un telefono**	*oon te-le-foh-no*

HEALTH AND EMERGENCY

Help!	**Aiuto!**	*a-yoo-to*
I am sick	**Mi sento male**	*mee sen-to ma-lay*
I am hurt	**Mi sono fatto male**	*mee son-no fat-to ma-lay*
I need...	**Ho bisogno di...**	*o bee-zon-yo dee*
the hospital	**l'ospedale**	*los-pe-da-lay*
a doctor	**un medico**	*oon me-dee-ko*
an ambulance	**un'ambulanza**	*oon am-boo-lant-sa*
the police	**la polizia**	*la po-leet-see-a*
medicine	**medicina**	*me-dee-chee-nah*

EATING

I would like...	**Vorrei...**	*vor-ray*
a table for two	**un tavolo per due**	*oon ta-vo-lo payr doo-ay*
the menu	**il menù**	*eel me-noo*
breakfast	**la colazione**	*la ko-lats-yo-nay*
lunch	**pranzare**	*pron-tsar-ay*
dinner	**cenare**	*chey-nar-ay*
the bill	**il conto**	*eel kon-to*
nonsmoking	**non-fumatore**	*non foo-ma-to-ray*
a drink	**una bibite**	*oon-a bee-bee-tay*
a glass of...	**un bicchiere di...**	*oon beek-ye-ray dee*
water	**acqua**	*ak-wa*
beer	**birra**	*beer-ra*
wine	**vino**	*vee-no*
I am...	**Sono...**	*so-no*
a vegetarian	**vegetariano/a**	*ve-jay-ta-ree-a-no/a*
diabetic	**diabetico/a**	*dee-a-be-tee-ko/a*
allergic	**allergico/a**	*al-ler-jee-ko/a*
kosher	**kosher**	*ko-shur*

SHOPPING

Do you have...?	**Avete...?**	*a-vet-ay*
Where can I buy...?	**Dove posso comprare...?**	*do-vay pos-so kom-pra-ray*
May I try this?	**Potrei provarlo?**	*po-tray pro-var-lo*
How much is this?	**Quanto costa?**	*kwan-to kos-ta*
cash	**in contanti**	*een kon-tan-tee*
credit card	**la carta di credito**	*la kar-ta dee kre-dee-to*
Too...	**Troppo...**	*trohp-po*
small	**piccolo/a**	*peek-ko-lo/a*
large	**grande**	*gran-day*
expensive	**caro**	*ka-ro*

TIME

What time is it?	**Che ora sono?**	*kay or-a so-no*
It is...	**Sono...**	*so-no*
eight o'clock	**le otto**	*lay oht-toh*
half past ten	**le dieci e mezza**	*lay dee-ay-chee ay med-za*
noon	**mezzogiorno**	*med-zo jor-no*
midnight	**mezzanotte**	*med-za-noht-tay*
during the day	**durante il giorno**	*doo-ran-tay eel jor-no*
in the morning	**di mattina**	*dee mat-tee-na*
in the afternoon	**nel pomeriggio**	*nel po-may-reed-jo*
in the evening	**la sera**	*la say-ra*
at night	**a notte**	*a not-tay*

DAYS OF THE WEEK

Monday	**lunedì**	*lee-ne-dee*
Tuesday	**martedì**	*mar-te-dee*
Wednesday	**mercoledì**	*mair-ko-le-dee*
Thursday	**giovedì**	*jo-ve-dee*
Friday	**venerdì**	*ven-air-dee*
Saturday	**sabato**	*sa-ba-toh*
Sunday	**domenica**	*do-me-nee-ka*
this week	**questa settimana**	*kwesta set-tee-ma-na*
this weekend	**questo fine settimana**	*kwest-o fi-nay set-tee-ma-na*
today	**oggi**	*oj-jee*
tomorrow	**domani**	*do-ma-nee*
yesterday	**ieri**	*yair-ee*

MONTHS

January	**gennaio**	*jen-na-yo*
February	**febbraio**	*feb-bra-yo*
March	**marzo**	*mart-zo*
April	**aprile**	*a-pree-lay*
May	**maggio**	*maj-jo*
June	**giugno**	*joon-yo*
July	**luglio**	*lool-yo*
August	**agosto**	*a-gos-toh*
September	**settembre**	*set-tem-bray*
October	**ottobre**	*ot-to-bray*
November	**novembre**	*no-vem-bray*
December	**dicembre**	*dee-chem-bray*
this month	**questo mese**	*kwest-o me-se*
this year	**quest'anno**	*kwest-an-no*
winter	**inverno**	*een-vair-no*
spring	**primavera**	*pree-ma-vair-a*
summer	**estate**	*es-ta-tay*
fall	**autunno**	*ow-toon-no*

NUMBERS

zero	**zero**	*dze-ro*
one	**uno**	*oo-no*
two	**due**	*doo-ay*
three	**tre**	*tray*
four	**quattro**	*kwat-troh*
five	**cinque**	*cheen-kway*
six	**sei**	*se-ee*
seven	**sette**	*set-tay*
eight	**otto**	*ot-toh*
nine	**nove**	*no-vay*
10	**dieci**	*dyay-chee*
11	**undici**	*oon-dee-chee*
12	**dodici**	*do-dee-chee*
13	**tredici**	*tray-dee-chee*
14	**quattordici**	*kwat-tor-dee-chee*
15	**quindici**	*kween-dee-chee*
16	**sedici**	*se-dee-chee*
17	**diciasette**	*dee-chias-set-tay*
18	**diciotto**	*dee-chiot-to*
19	**dicianove**	*dee-chian-no-vay*
20	**venti**	*ven-tee*
100	**cento**	*chen-toh*
1,000	**mile**	*meel-lay*

STREET INDEX

A

Abruzzi, Via: Map 4 B2

Acaia, Via: Overview Map E5

Acciaioli, Via: Map 7 D5

Acilio, Clivo di: Map 5 C3

Acquasparta, Via degli: Map 2 A2

Adriana, Piazza: Map 7 B5

Aganoor Pompili, Viale Vittoria: Map 3 A4

Agliardi, Via Cardinal: Map 7 D2

Agnello, Via dell': Map 5 C3

Agnesi, Largo Gaetana: Map 5 C3

Alberico II, Via: Map 7 B5

Alberteschi, Lungotevere: Map 6 B5

Alberto, Via Carlo: Overview Map D5; Map 4 F4; Map 5 B5

Aleardi, Via: Map 5 E6

Alessandria, Piazza: Map 4 B5

Alessandrina, Via: Overview Map D4; Map 4 A5; Map 5 C2

Alessandrino, Via Clemente: Map 7 E2

Alessandro III, Via: Map 7 D2

Alfieri, Via: Map 5 D6

Alibert, Via: Map 3 C4

Altoviti, Lungotevere degli: Map 7 C5

Amatriciani, Vicolo degli: Map 2 A1

Amba Aradam, Via dell': Map 5 F5

Amendola, Via Giovanni: Map 4 E4; Map 5 A5

Ancona, Via: Map 4 B5

Angelico, Borgo: Map 7 B4

Angelico, Viale: Overview Map A2

Anguillara, Lungotevere degli: Map 6 B4

Anicia, Via: Map 6 C4

Aniene, Via: Map 4 B4

Annia, Via: Map 5 E4

Annibaldi, Via degli: Map 5 C3

Annibaliano, Piazza: Overview Map A6

Annunzio, Viale Gabriele d': Map 3 A3

Appia Antica, Via: Overview Map F5

Appia Nuova, Via: Overview Map E6

Aquila, Vicolo dell': Map 1 B2

Aquiro, Via in: Map 2 B5

Aracoeli, Via D': Map 1 C6

Aradam, Via dell'Amba: Overview Map E5

Ara Massima di Ercole, Via dell': Map 5 E1

Arancio, Via dell': Map 3 D3

Ara Pacis, Via: Map 3 C2

Arcaccio, Vicolo dell': Map 1 D1

Archetto, Via dell': Map 5 A1

Arcione, Via in: Map 3 F6

Arco Acetari: Map 1 B1

Arco degli Acquasparta: Map 2 A2

Arco dei Ginnasi, Via dell': Map 1 C5

Arco della Ciambella, Via: Map 1 B4

Arco della Pace, Via dell': Map 2 B1

Arco del Monte, Via dell': Map 1 D2

Arco di Parma, Via: Map 2 A1

Arco di San Calisto, Via dell': Map 6 B3

Arenula, Largo: Map 1 C4

Arenula, Via: Overview Map D3; Map 1 E3

Argilla, Via dell': Map 7 E1

Ariosto, Via Ludovico: Map 5 D6

Armellini, Via: Map 6 E1

Armi, Lungotevere delle: Overview Map B2

Arnaldo Da Brescia, Lungotevere: Overview Map B3

Artisti, Via degli: Map 4 C1

Ascanio, Via D': Map 3 F2

Astalli, Via degli: Map 1 B6

Atleta, Vicolo: Map 6 C5

Augusta, Lungotevere in: Overview Map B3; Map 3 D2

Augusto Imperatore, Piazza: Map 3 D3

Aurelia, Via: Map 7 D2

Aurelia Antica, Via: Overview Map D1

Aureliana, Via: Map 4 C3

Aurelio, Via Marco: Map 5 E4

Aventino, Lungotevere: Overview Map E3; Map 6 D5

Aventino, Viale: Overview Map E4; Map 5 F2

Avignonesi, Via degli: Map 4 D1

Azeglio, Via Massimo d': Map 4 E4; Map 5 A5

B

Babuccio, Vicolo del: Map 5 A2

Babuino, Via del: Overview Map B3; Map 3 C4

Babuino, Vicolo del: Map 3 B3

Baccelli, Viale Guido: Overview Map E4, F4; Map 5 F3

Baccina, Via: Map 5 C3

Bachelet, Via: Map 4 D5

Balbo, Via Cesare: Map 4 E3; Map 5 A4

Balestrari, Via dei: Map 1 C2

Bambini, Viale dei: Map 3 A4

Capponi, Piazza Americo: Map 7 B4

Cappuccini, Via: Map 4 D1

Capranica, Piazza: Map 2 B5

Caprareccia, Via: Map 4 F3; Map 5 B4

Caprettari, Piazza dei: Map 1 A4

Capua, Via Raimondo Da: Map 6 E6

Caracciolo, Via Francesco: Map 7 A1

Carcani, Via Michele: Map 6 E3

Cardelli, Piazza: Map 3 E2

Cardello, Via: Map 5 C3

Carducci, Via Giosuè: Map 4 C3

Carine, Via delle: Map 5 C3

Caro, Via Lucrezio: Map 7 A6

Carrette, Via: Map 5 C2

Carrozze, Via del: Map 3 D4

Casilina, Via: Overview Map D6

Casini, Via Filippo: Map 6 D1

Cassiodoro, Via: Map 7 B5

Castelfidardo, Via: Map 4 C5

Castello, Lungotevere: Overview Map C2; Map 7 C6

Castro Pretorio, Via: Map 4 E6

Castro Pretorio, Viale: Map 4 C6

Catalana, Via: Map 1 E5; Map 6 A5

Catania, Via: Overview Map B6

Catinari, Vicolo dei: Map 1 D3

Catone, Via: Map 7 A3

Cattaneo, Via Carlo: Map 4 F5; Map 5 B5

Catullo, Via: Map 7 A5

Cava Aurelia, Via della: Map 7 F1

Cavaletti, Via: Map 1 D6

Cavalieri del Santo Sepolcro, Via dei: Map 7 C4

Cavalieri di Malta, Piazza dei: Map 6 E5

Cavalli Marini, Viale dei: Map 4 A2

Cavallini, Via Pietro: Map 3 D1

Cavour, Piazza: Overview Map C2; Map 7 B6

Cavour, Via: Overview Map C5, D4; Map 4 E4, F3; Map 5 A5, B4, C3

Cecchi, Via Antonio: Map 6 F4

Cedro, Vicolo del: Map 6 B1

Celimontana, Piazza: Map 5 E4

Celimontana, Via: Map 5 D4

Celsa, Via: Map 1 C6

Cenci, Arco dei: Map 1 E4

Cenci, Lungotevere dei: Overview Map D3; Map 1 F5; Map 6 A5

Cenci, Piazza: Map 1 E3

Cenci, Vicolo Beatrice: Map 1 E3; Map 6 A4

Cenci, Vicolo dei: Map 1 E3

Cerchi, Via dei: Overview Map E4; Map 5 D1, E2

Ceriani, Via Antonio: Map 7 F1

Cernaia, Via: Overview Map C5; Map 4 C4

Cerveteri, Via: Overview Map E6

Cesare, Viale Giulio: Overview Map B2; Map 7 A3

Cestari, Via dei: Map 1 B5

Ceste, Vicolo delle: Map 1 A5

Chiana, Via: Overview Map A5

Chiavari, Largo dei: Map 1 B3

Chiavari, Via dei: Map 1 C3

Chiesa Nuova, Piazza della: Map 7 E6

Chigi, Largo: Map 2 A6; Map 3 F4

Chiodaroli, Vicolo dei: Map 1 C3

Cialdini, Via Enrico: Map 4 F5; Map 5 B6

Ciancaleoni, Via: Map 5 B3

Cicerone, Via: Overview Map B2; Map 7 B6

Cilicia, Via: Overview Map F5

Cimarra, Via: Map 4 F2; Map 5 B3

Cinque, Vicolo de: Map 6 A2

Cinquecento, Piazza dei: Map 4 E4

Cinque Lune, Piazza: Map 2 A3

Cinque Scole, Piazza de: Map 1 E4

Cipresso, Via del: Map 6 A2

Cipro, Via: Overview Map B1

Circo Massimo, Via del: Overview Map E4; Map 5 F2

Cisterna, Via della: Map 6 B3

Civitavecchia, Via: Map 4 A5

Claudia, Via: Overview Map D4; Map 5 E4

Clementina, Via: Map 5 B3

Clementino, Via di: Map 3 E2

Clodia, Circonvallazione: Overview Map A1, B1

Clodio, Piazzale: Overview Map B1

Cola di Rienzo, Piazza: Overview Map B2; Map 7 A6

Cola di Rienzo, Via: Overview Map B2; Map 7 A5

Collegio Capranica, Via del: Map 2 A5

Collegio Romano, Piazza del: Map 1 A6; Map 2 C6; Map 5 A1

Collegio Romano, Via del: Map 2 C6; Map 5 A1

Collina, Via: Map 4 C4

Colonnelle, Via delle: Map 2 B5

Colonna Antonina, Via della: Map 2 A6

Colonna, Galleria di Piazza: Map 3 F4

Colonna, Piazza: Map 2 A6; Map 3 F4

Colonna, Via Vittoria: Map 3 D1

Colonnette, Via: Map 3 C3

Ferro di Cavallo, Piazza del: Map 3 C2

Ferruccio, Via: Map 5 C6

Fiammetta, Piazza: Map 2 A2

Fico, Piazza del: Map 2 B1

Fico, Vicolo del: Map 2 B1

Fienaroli, Via dei: Map 6 C3

Fienili, Via dei: Map 5 D1

Filiberto, Via Emanuele: Overview Map D5; Map 5 D6

Filipperi, Via Bartolomeo: Map 6 B3

Filippini, Via dei: Map 7 D6

Fiorentini, Lungotevere dei: Map 7 D5

Firenze, Via: Map 4 E3; Map 5 A4

Fiume, Piazza: Map 4 B4

Fiume, Via del: Map 3 B2

Flaminia, Via: Overview Map B3

Flaminio, Lungotevere: Overview Map A3

Flavia, Via: Map 4 C4

Florida, Via: Map 1 C4

Fontana, Via Domenico: Map 5 E6

Fontanella, Via della: Map 3 B3

Fontanella di Borghese, Largo della: Map 3 E2, E3

Fontanella di Borghese, Via della: Map 3 E3

Fonte di Fauno, Via della: Map 5 F2

Foraggi, Via dei: Map 5 D1

Fori Imperiali, Via dei: Overview Map D4; Map 5 C2

Fornaci, Via delle: Map 7 E3, F3

Fornari, Via dei: Map 5 B1

Foro Olitorio, Via del: Map 6 B6

Foscolo, Via: Map 5 C6

Fossa, Via della: Map 2 B1

Fosse di Castello, Via delle: Map 7 B5

Frangipane, Via: Map 5 C3

Frasche, Via delle: Map 5 B3

Fratte di Trastevere, Via delle: Map 6 C3

Frattina, Via: Map 3 D4

Frezza, Via della: Map 3 C3

Friuli, Via: Map 4 C2

Frosinone, Via: Map 4 A5

Frusta, Vicolo della: Map 6 B1

Funari, Via dei: Map 1 D5

GH

Gaeta, Via: Map 4 C5

Galeno, Piazza: Overview Map B5; Map 4 B6

Galilei, Via: Map 5 D6

Galletti, Via Bartolomeo: Map 6 C1

Gallia, Via: Overview Map E5

Gallinaccio, Vicolo del: Map 3 E6

Gallo, Vicolo di: Map 1 B1

Gambero, Via del: Map 3 E4

Garibaldi, Via: Map 6 A1, C1

Garofano, Via del: Map 5 C3

Gasperi, Via Alcide de: Map 7 D2

Gatta, Via della: Map 5 B1

Gelsomini, Viale Manlio: Overview Map E3

Gelsomino, Via del: Map 7 E1

Genova, Via: Map 4 E2; Map 5 A3

Genovesi, Via dei: Map 6 C5

Gensola, Via: Map 6 B5

Germanico, Via: Map 7 A4

Gessi, Via Romolo: Map 6 F4

Gesù, Piazza del: Map 1 C6

Gesù, Via del: Map 1 B6

Gesù e Maria, Via di: Map 3 B3

Gianicolense, Circonvallazione: Overview Map F2

Gianicolense, Lungotevere: Overview Map C2; Map 7 E5

Gianicolo, Passeggiata di: Overview Map D2; Map 7 E4

Gianicolo, Via del: Map 7 D4, E4

Gianniti, Via: Map 6 E2

Giardini, Via dei: Map 4 D1

Giardino Theodoli, Via del: Map 3 E3

Gigli d'Oro, Via dei: Map 3 F1; Map 2 A3

Giglio, Vicolo del: Map 1 C1

Gioberti, Via: Map 4 F4; Map 5 A5

Giolitti, Via Giovanni: Overview Map C5; Map 4 F5; Map 5 B6

Giotto, Viale: Overview Map E4

Giubbonari, Via dei: Map 1 D2

Giulia, Via: Map 7 E5, F6

Giuliana, Via della: Overview Map B1

Giusti, Via: Map 5 C6

Giustiniani, Via: Map 2 B4

Glorioso, Viale: Map 6 D2

Goethe, Viale: Map 4 B1

Goito, Via: Map 4 C4

Goldoni, Largo Carlo: Map 3 D3

Governo Vecchio, Via del: Map 2 C1; Map 7 D6

Gracchi, Via dei: Map 7 A5

Granari, Via: Map 2 C2

Grazie, Via delle: Map 7 B3

Grazioli, Piazza: Map 1 B6

Greca, Via della: Map 5 E1

Greci, Via dei: Map 3 C4

Gregoriana, Via: Map 3 D6

Gregorio VII, Via: Overview Map D1; Map 7 E1

Grillo, Salita del: Map 5 B2

Giovanni: Map 5 D5

Pasquino, Piazza di: Map 1 A2; Map 2 C2

Pasquino, Via di: Map 1 A2

Paste, Via delle: Map 2 B5

Pastini, Via dei: Map 2 B5

Pastrengo, Via: Map 4 D3

Pateras, Via: Map 6 D1

Pelagio, Via: Map 7 D3

Pellegrino, Via del: Map 1 B1; Map 7 E6

Pelliccia, Via della: Map 6 B2

Penitenza, Via della: Map 7 F5

Penitenza, Vicolo della: Map 7 F5

Penna, Via della: Map 3 B2

Peretti, Via Pietro: Map 6 C5

Petrarca, Via: Map 5 C6

Petroselli, Via: Overview Map D3; Map 5 D1

Pettinari, Via dei: Map 1 D2

Pfeiffer, Via Padre Pancrazio: Map 7 C4

Piacenza, Via: Map 4 E2; Map 5 A3

Pianellari, Via dei: Map 2 A3; Map 3 F1

Piave, Via: Map 4 C4

Piede, Vicolo del: Map 6 B2

Piè di Marmo, Via: Map 1 A6

Piemonte, Via: Map 4 C3

Pierleoni, Lungotevere dei: Map 1 F5

Pietà, Via della: Map 1 D2

Pietra, Piazza di: Map 2 B6

Pietra, Via di: Map 2 B6

Pietro della Valle, Via: Map 7 B5

Pigna, Piazza della: Map 1 A5

Pigna, Via della: Map 1 A5

Pilotta, Piazza della: Map 5 A2

Pilotta, Via della: Map 5 B2

Pinciana, Via: Overview Map B4; Map 4 A2

Pincinula, Piazza in: Map 6 B5

Pio, Borgo: Map 7 B4

Pio X, Via: Map 7 B3

Pio XII, Piazza: Map 7 C3

Piombo, Vicolo del: Map 5 B1

Piramide Cestia, Viale del: Overview Map E3

Pisani, Via Vittor: Map 7 A1

Piscinula, Via in: Map 6 B5

Pistrucci, Via Benedetto: Map 3 C1

Plauto, Via: Map 7 B4

Plebiscito, Via del: Map 1 B6; Map 5 B1

Plinio, Via: Map 7 A5

Po, Via: Overview Map A5; Map 4 A3

Polacchi, Via dei: Map 1 D6

Poli, Via: Map 3 F5

Policlinico, Via: Overview Map B5

Policlinico, Viale del: Overview Map C5; Map 4 C6

Politeama, Via del: Map 6 A3

Poliziano, Via Angelo: Map 5 C5

Pollarola, Piazza: Map 1 B2

Polo, Viale Marco: Overview Map F4

Polveriera, Via della: Map 5 C3

Polverone, Vicolo del: Map 1 D1

Pompieri, Via dei: Map 1 D2

Ponte Cavour: Map 3 D1

Ponte Cestio: Map 6 B5

Ponte Fabricio: Map 1 F5; Map 6 A5

Ponte Garibaldi: Map 1 F3; Map 6 A4

Ponte Giuseppe Mazzini: Map 7 E5

Ponte Palatino: Map 6 C6

Ponte Principe Amedeo Savoia Aosta: Map 7 D5

Ponte Regina

Margherita: Map 3 B1

Ponte Rotto, Via di: Map 6 C5

Ponte Sant'Angelo: Map 7 C6

Ponte Sisto: Map 1 E1; Map 6 A3

Ponte Sisto, Via di: Map 6 A2

Ponte Sublicio: Map 6 E4

Ponte Vittorio Emanuele II: Map 7 C5

Pontefici, Via dei: Map 3 C3

Popolo, Piazza del: Overview Map B3; Map 3 A2

Porcari, Via Stefano: Map 7 B4

Porta Angelica, Via di: Map 7 B3

Porta Capena, Piazza di: Map 5 F2

Porta Castello, Via: Map 7 B5

Porta Cavalleggeri, Via: Map 7 D2

Porta Fabbrica, Via di: Map 7 D2

Porta Lavernale, Via di: Map 6 F5

Porta Metronia, Piazza di: Map 5 F4

Porta Pia, Piazzale di: Map 4 B5

Porta Pinciana, Via di: Map 3 C6; Map 4 C1

Porta Portese, Piazza di: Map 6 E4

Porta Portese, Via di: Map 6 E3

Porta San Sebastiano, Via di: Overview Map E5

Portico d'Ottavia, Via del: Map 1 E5; Map 6 A6

Porto Fluviale, Via del: Overview Map F3

Porto, Via del: Map 6 D5

Portoghesi, Via dei: Map 3 F1

Portuense, Lungotevere: Overview Map E2

Portuense, Via: Overview Map E2; Map 6 E3

Posta, Via della: Map 7 B3

San Bernardo, Piazza: Map 4 D3

San Bernardo, Via di: Map 5 B1

San Calisto, Piazza: Map 6 B3

San Claudio, Piazza: Map 3 F4

San Claudio, Via: Map 3 F4

San Cosimato, Piazza: Map 6 C2

San Cosimato, Via: Map 6 C2

San Crisogono, Via: Map 6 C4

San Croce in Gerusalemme, Via di: Overview Map D6

San Domenico, Via: Map 6 E6

San Francesco a Ripa, Via di: Map 6 C3

San Francesco a Ripa, Vicolo: Map 6 D3

San Francesco d'Assisi, Piazza: Map 6 D3

San Francesco di Paola, Piazza: Map 5 C3

San Francesco di Sales, Via di: Map 7 F4

San Francesco di Sales, Vicolo di: Map 7 F4

San Gallicano, Via: Map 6 B3

San Giacomo, Via: Map 3 C3

San Giosafat, Via: Map 5 F1

San Giovanni d'Arco, Via: Map 2 B3

San Giovanni de Matha, Piazza: Map 6 B4

San Giovanni Decollato, Via: Map 5 D1

San Giovanni in Laterano, Piazza: Map 5 E6

San Giovanni in Laterano, Via di: Overview Map D5; Map 5 D4

San Giuseppe Calasanzio, Via: Map 1 A2

San Giuseppe Labre, Via: Map 5 B3

San Gregorio, Via di: Overview Map D4; Map 5 E3

San Liberio, Via: Map 7 E3

San Lorenzo in Lucina, Piazza: Map 3 E3

San Macuto, Piazza di: Map 2 B6

San Marcelio, Piazza: Map 2 C7

San Marcello, Via: Map 2 C7; Map 5 A1

San Marco, Via: Map 5 B1

San Martino ai Monti, Piazza: Map 5 C4

San Martino ai Monti, Via: Map 5 B5

San Martino della Battaglia, Via: Map 4 D5

San Michele, Via di: Map 6 D4

San Nicola da Tolentino, Salita di: Map 4 D2

San Nicola da Tolentino, Via: Map 4 D2

San Nicola dei Cesarini, Via: Map 1 C5

San Pancrazio, Via di: Overview Map E1

San Pantaleo, Piazza di: Map 1 B2

San Pantaleo, Via di: Map 1 A2

San Paolo alla Regola, Piazza di: Map 1 E2

San Paolo alla Regola, Via di: Map 1 D2

San Paolo del Brasile, Viale: Map 4 B1

San Paolo della Croce, Via: Map 5 E4

San Pellegrino, Via del: Map 7 B3

San Pietro in Carcere, Via: Map 5 C1

San Pietro in Vincoli, Piazza: Map 5 C3

San Pietro, Piazza: Overview Map C1; Map 7 C3

San Pio X, Via: Map 7 C5

San Salvatore in Campo, Piazza: Map 1 D2

San Salvatore in

Campo, Via: Map 1 D2

San Sebastianello, Via: Map 3 C5

San Silvestro, Piazza: Map 3 E3

San Simeone, Piazza: Map 2 A1

San Spirito, Borgo: Overview Map C2

San Telesforo, Via: Map 7 E3

San Teodoro, Via di: Map 5 D1

San Tullio, Via: Map 4 C4

San Venanzio, Via: Map 5 C1

San Vitale, Via: Map 4 E2; Map 5 A3

San Vito, Via: Map 5 B5

Sangallo, Lungotevere dei: Overview Map C2; Map 7 E5

Sannio, Via: Map 5 F6

Sant'Agata dei Goti, Via: Map 5 B3

Sant'Agostino, Piazza di: Map 3 F1

Sant'Alberto Magno, Via: Map 5 F1

Sant'Alessio, Via di: Map 6 F6

Sant'Andrea delle Fratte, Via di: Map 3 E5

Sant'Angelo, Borgo: Map 7 C5

Sant'Angelo in Pescheria, Via: Map 1 E5

Sant'Agnese in Agone, Via di: Map 2 B2

Sant'Agostino, Piazza di: Map 2 A3

Sant'Agostino, Via di: Map 2 A3

Santamaura, Via: Map 7 A2

Sant'Ambrogio, Via: Map 1 E5

Sant'Andrea della Valle, Piazza: Map 1 B3

Sant'Anna, Via di: Map 1 C4

Sant'Anselmo, Via di: Map 6 F6

Sant'Apollinare, Piazza di: Map 2 A2

Sant'Egidio, Piazza: Map 6 B2

INDEX

RESTAURANTS INDEX

NIGHTLIFE INDEX

SHOPS INDEX

HOTELS INDEX

CONTRIBUTORS TO THE SECOND EDITION

JUDY EDELHOFF   *A Day in Rome, Sights, Museums and Galleries, Performing Arts, Hotels*
Judy Edelhoff, a native Floridian, has written about art, food, archaeology, wine, and customs in Italy for *Italy Daily* (by the *International Herald Tribune*) and *The American Magazine*. In other adventures, she has picked grapes, wild mushrooms, and saffron in the Italian countryside.

ANGELA ELLIS   *Introduction, Neighborhoods, Restaurants, Shops*
Angela Ellis is a former network television news producer, currently working as a freelance writer and producer in Rome, where she has lived since 2003.

BRENDAN MONAGHAN   *Nightlife, Recreation, City Essentials*
Brendan Monaghan is originally from New York. He has been living in Rome since 2002 and works as an information technology consultant and freelance writer.

OTHER CONTRIBUTORS
Alexei Cohen (Sights – Commemorative Plaques)

CONTRIBUTORS TO THE FIRST EDITION
Kim Westerman, Kristine Crane

PHOTO CREDITS

© Angela Ellis: page III, Excelsior; page XII, Hassler; Map 4, Excelsior; page 26, Caffè Sant'Eustachio; page 26, Myosotis; page 28, La Rosetta; page 28, Gina; page 36, Insalata Ricca; page 38, Lettere Café; page 43, Big Mama; page 43, Chakra Café; page 45, Lettere Café; page 45, Stardust; page 50, Berté; page 63, Museo Barracco di Scultura Antica; page 65, Galleria Dell'Accademia di San Luca; page 69, Galleria Nazionale D'Arte Moderna; page 73, Santa Maria Degli Angeli; page 79, Excelsior; page 81, Hotel Tiziano; page 81, Dei Borgognoni; page 83, Hotel de Russie; page 83, Hassler Villa Medici; page 83, Locarno; page 85, Excelsior; page 85, St. Regis Grand; page 87, Atlante Star

All other photos: © Phil Shipman

MOON METRO ROME
SECOND EDITION

Avalon Travel Publishing
An Imprint of Avalon Publishing Group, Inc.

Text and maps © 2006 by Avalon Travel Publishing
All rights reserved.

Grateful acknowledgment is made for reproduction permission: ATAC
S.p.A: Rome Metro Map © 2005

Some photos and illustrations are used by permission and are the
property of the original copyright owners.

ISBN-10: 1-56691-941-X
ISBN-13: 978-1-56691-941-8
ISSN: 1543-1908

Editor and Series Manager: Grace Fujimoto
Design: Jacob Goolkasian
Map Design: Mike Morgenfeld, Suzanne Service
Production Coordinators: Amber Pirker, Jacob Goolkasian
Graphics Coordinator: Stefano Boni
Cartographer: Suzanne Service
Map Editor: Kat Smith
Indexer (Street Index): Naomi Adler Dancis
Proofreader: Kate McKinley
Front cover photos: Front cover photos: motorcycle, Via del Corso, © Franz-
Marc Frei/CORBIS; Castel Sant'Angelo, © Digital Vision/Getty Images

Printed in China through Colorcraft Ltd., Hong Kong
Printing History
1st edition – 2003
2nd edition – April 2006
5 4 3 2 1

Please send all feedback about this book to:

Moon Metro Rome
Avalon Travel Publishing
1400 65th Street, Suite 250
Emeryville, CA 94608, USA
email: atpfeedback@avalonpub.com
website: www.moon.com

Moon Metro and the Moon logo are the property of Avalon Travel
Publishing, an imprint of Avalon Publishing Group. All other marks
and logos depicted are the property of the original owners. All rights
reserved. No part of this book may be translated or reproduced in any
form, except brief extracts by a reviewer for the purpose of a review,
without written permission of the copyright owner.

Although every effort was made to ensure that the information was
correct at the time of going to press, the publisher does not assume
and hereby disclaims any liability to any party for any loss or damage
caused by errors, omissions, or any potential travel disruption due to
labor or financial difficulty, whether such errors or omissions result
from negligence, accident, or any other cause.

Covering eighteen major cities throughout the world, MOON METRO takes travel to a new level with its innovative fusion of discreet maps and insider advice.

AMSTERDAM

BARCELONA

BERLIN

LONDON

MONTRÉAL

PARIS

ROME

TORONTO

VANCOUVER

**AVAILABLE AT BOOKSTORES AND
THROUGH ONLINE BOOKSELLERS**

Also available from
MOON METRO

BOSTON

LOS ANGELES

MIAMI

CHICAGO

LAS VEGAS

NEW YORK CITY

SAN FRANCISCO

SEATTLE

WASHINGTON D.C.

www.moon.com

metro e ferrovie metropolitane/*metro and*